UNFINISHED WORK

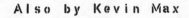

Also by Kevin Max

At the Foot of Heaven
Jesus Freaks (dc Talk and the Voice of the Martyrs)

and

His solo CD, *Stereotype Be*
(Forefront Records, 2001)

www.KevinMax.com

UNFINISHED WORK

Kevin Max

THOMAS NELSON PUBLISHERS®
Nashville

A Division of Thomas Nelson, Inc.
www.ThomasNelson.com

Published in Nashville, Tennessee, by Thomas Nelson, Inc.

ISBN 0-7852-6630-5

Printed in the United States of America

To Max and Elaine Smith

"And the one who
wanders is not lost."

J. R. R. Tolkien,
The Lord of the Rings

CONTENTS

SOUND CHECK

SOUND
CHECK

Ask most any artist to explain what he does—why he writes music, what it means, how he does it—and you're likely to get the same five-word answer: "The song says it all."

It's understandable. Writing songs, making records, standing on a stage and singing your heart out—they're personal forms of expression. And the best music, the most honest and up front, encapsulates the essence of the person who created it. It's a mirror held up to an artist's soul, a way of being real, exposing your deepest thoughts and feelings, and that shouldn't need any further explanation.

If a song touches a listener, stirs something in the spirit, or makes a connection that rings true, that's all anyone really needs to know. A song that succeeds in saying what the artist truly intends is one of the best, most complete, and most satisfying forms of communication God has given us. A song really can "say it all."

But I also understand why audiences and fans want to know what's behind the music that moves them. We've all had that magical moment: we hear the lyrics and melody, and it's as if suddenly someone is singing exactly how we feel, what we think or believe, hope or fear. A right song at the right time speaks for us in a way that maybe we can't, summing up perfectly the unique mix of emotion and experience, passion and perplexity, that makes us who we are. "How did he know?" is the question we find ourselves asking when we hear a song that puts into words and notes the truth of who we are and who we want to be. Considering the incredible ability of music to reach us and teach us, it's no wonder we're curious about how that miracle is accomplished.

That is why I wanted to write this book.

The Story Behind the Song

I've been a songwriter and musician most of my life. I know the power and the responsibility that come with the gift. I can't count all the times fans and friends have told me that a track on an album or a song in a concert meant something special to them. In those moments, the look they give me is one full of expectation, as if they're waiting for me to reveal how I could stare into their lives and make music out of what I found there. And I always feel that I've disappointed them a little when I shrug and smile and tell them, "The song says it all."

It's true. The song *does* say it all if it's honest and from the heart and drawn from real life. Maybe that just means we all share more than we imagine; everybody is connected by common chords, musical and otherwise, that we can recognize when they're touched.

But I also think it means that there really *is* a story behind every song. Music stands on its own, but it doesn't exist in a vacuum. Artists draw inspiration every day from what they see around them and what they feel inside. The circumstances and situations sparking that inspiration explain a lot about the person who sings the song as well as the one who is listening. I've heard it said that context is everything, and I believe it. The right song at the right time can change a person's life. But no one's life can be summed up in a song. Music, at its best, can be the expression of a person's individual reality. Maybe knowing a little of the history—what went into the message and meaning of a song—could help others who are trying to make sense of their lives, just like that artist.

When I first had the idea for this book, I knew I wanted to say many things. The story of my life, from being an adopted baby to becoming one-third of a major musical attraction called dc Talk, is as much a part of me as the music I've been making for most of those years. I've had more than my share of high drama and low comedy, surreal situations and conflicting conditions. Searching for my birth parents, finding my voice in dc Talk, learning to live with the woman I love from the perspective of a husband and friend, keeping hold of my soul in the music industry big leagues, and most important, trying to stay true to my faith in Jesus Christ—I have been on a wild ride. And it's not over yet.

The more I thought about it, and the more I prayed about it, the more I realized that the key to this book could be found in the lifelong challenge that I've faced—that we've all faced—to be true to myself as the person God created me to be. We're all fearfully and wonderfully made, as Psalm 139 tells us. We've all been given unique gifts and talents. We all have an extraordinary destiny to work out day by day. Keeping our eyes fixed on that higher calling; not letting anything stand between us and the fulfillment of that promise; staying focused, battling compromise, rejecting labels and categories and the way we're told it has to be—that's what my life and my music have been about. And that's what this book is about.

> "We're all fearfully and wonderfully made. We've all been given unique gifts and talents. We all have an extraordinary destiny to work out day by day."

Be

If there's one theme that constantly recurs in the chronicle of my life and music, and in the pages of this book, it's that all of us are works in progress. That is why I've used the title *Unfinished Work*. God is calling us to be totally ourselves, fully free, liberated to become the persons He intended when He called each of us by name in the mother's womb, according to Galatians 1:15. Unfinished work. After everything

I've been through as a man in the modern world, as an artist with a calling, and as a witness to my faith, I keep falling back on that idea.

I'm not perfect, but I am struggling to be me. And I want to challenge you to be yourself. The story of our lives is incomplete, and God the Master Author will be shaping the plotline until our dying day.

Each one of us is a valuable force in the culture and in society. I want you to realize who you really are in God's eyes, but at the same time understand that, in order to find yourself, you sometimes have to go through trials and humiliation. We're all designed very differently, each with special gifts, and if we could start to use those gifts, we could be helpful to the world and to each other.

Finding yourself is never easy, and being in the public spotlight sometimes makes the process more difficult. I started out wanting to be a rock and roll star and eventually found myself in the middle of the contemporary Christian music world. I believe it was for a reason. I've been given a platform that has allowed me to say what I think is important, and it comes down to this very simple message: be yourself.

But I've noticed that the minute I try to be honest and real about who I am, some of my Christian brothers and sisters tend to become a bit nervous. I'm supposed to be one of their spokespeople, someone that kids look up to. I've been told that a lot of parents and youth leaders are concerned that I'm making the wrong impression, and to tell you the truth, if they knew what goes on inside my brain sometimes, they'd *really* be worried. Isn't that true of everyone? We're fallen creatures, the Bible tells us, and we need salvation and redemption.

Basically I'm no different from you. I just happen to be an entertainer who wants to challenge people with words and music. I would like to be able to open Christians' minds a bit more to the realities outside their closed culture. I'd like to let people know that God is bigger than the church, bigger than four walls, and I think that's one of the messages I've been called to impart. I must go as far as I can into mainstream society, into mass culture, speaking the truth to as wide an audience as possible. And when I do that, some people become uncomfortable.

Recently people who question my behavior and attitude have attacked me on the Internet. They don't like the fact that I have one of the only chat sites (www.kevinmax.com) with no parental controls, one that allows anybody at all to voice his opinion. Of course, there are going to be a few people who will log on and say things for sheer shock value, but that's the price of freedom. I've left myself open to paying that price. It doesn't stop there, however. People have labeled me Christian music's bad boy because I like to have a beer or a glass of wine once in a while. People hear rumors and gossip, and they assume the worst.

Christian Music's Bad Boy

My only answer to all their accusations is to say that if a bad boy is somebody who tries to think outside the box, then

I'm guilty as charged. I've never tried to deliberately alienate or anger people; I'm just being who I am, and I try to do it better each and every day. I learn from my mistakes and try to overcome my weaknesses. Maybe I like to push the boundaries, but I've tried to make sure I'm always pushing in a positive direction.

I've never felt the need to live up to the media's expectations, good or bad, and I refuse to become a caricature of myself. I've known a few performers who have gotten so twisted up in their images that they started to believe the hype and ended up like empty shells with nothing real inside. As Christians, we're called to have compassion for people who live in a godless existence without hope. The truth is that without a perfect Being in our lives, we become schizophrenic and full of rage.

Sometimes I get angry too. I feel an underlying tension of wanting to escape the voices telling me what to do and who I should be. I want people to know that they don't always have to listen to what others tell them to do. Each person should listen to what his soul is telling him to do, and if there is spiritual revelation in his life, he should listen to that. I want people to go deeper, and I think music is a great way to stir their minds and emotions. I'd like my audience to get more out of my songs than just a way to pass the time on the morning commute.

But at the same time I aim to please. One of my goals is to see people dancing to my music in a disco somewhere in Prague or Beijing, as much as to encourage them to sit alone

in their rooms at night reading the lyrics. Music creates a powerful link between human beings. It moves our souls in ways
that books or movies can't. For that reason I believe that
music should have a message. Personally I've always gotten the
most out of songs that take me to new places and make me
think about my life.

Examining who we are and why we're here makes life
interesting and motivates us to get the most out of it. We
should all relax a little and accept the fact that we aren't perfect and that we're striving to find truth and peace and a purpose to our lives. I believe that one of the primary purposes
of my life is to present truth through my music, but even
that can become a trap. Being a "Christian artist" is as much a
tag or a box or a package as any other title. A friend who makes
music happens to be a Buddhist. Yet no one calls what he does
"Buddhist music" or refers to him as a "Buddhist singer." People are more complex than
that, more multifaceted, and I don't know a single artist who
doesn't want to talk to as many people as possible, in as broad
a scope as he can encompass.

> "Examining who we are and why we're here makes life interesting and motivates us to get the most out of it."

You might be reading this and thinking, *If the shoe fits, wear
it.* As far as dc Talk goes, you would have a point. dc Talk
was founded on a premise of making accessible music with
Christian lyrics to stimulate the Christian mind and challenge

the non-Christian mind into wondering about the truth. So, for the band, that evangelical label isn't wrong. I've already been pinpointed as a member of dc Talk, and our audience already knows me by my profession of faith, but to constantly be identified only in that way can create a major obstacle. Why should I bother to try something different? Why not just stay where it's safe, within the group, and do what everyone has come to expect?

Looking for Answers

The answer is simple, but it's not easy. A bigger world out there needs to be engaged and entertained and explored. I enjoy hanging out with people who don't share my faith because I can have great conversations while my assumptions are being tested. Proverbs 27 states that iron sharpens iron. When you surround yourself with the same group of people all the time and you talk to each other in the same specialized language, you're not sharpening anything except your preconceptions. Without being questioned about what you believe, how can you know what you really stand for?

Talking to an atheist helps me to understand and defend what I believe. It helps me to delve deep. Where do I get my facts? Where does my theology come from? How did I form my worldview? These are the big questions.

You may respond, "The answers are in the Bible and in the church. That's as far as you need to look." Well, I'm a student of the Bible, and I have been for many years. I also attend church although, for me, the best church experience can be found in having a relationship with a group of believers, any-where and anytime. And like any other Christian, I have had my worldview shaped by Scripture and fellowship. The bottom line is that if I don't believe Scripture is the truth, then I don't know what truth is. It doesn't stop there, however. I've got to be able to defend what I believe, and that means allowing my faith to be weighed and measured by skeptics and doubters.

Let's face it. The Christian life requires all the faith we can muster. To believe that a Man actually could walk on water and be raised from the dead is to believe in things that most people will try to laugh off and call fairy tales or myths. But I've looked closely at the world around me, and I've come to the conviction that God is real. I believe in the reality of heaven and hell. That belief alone puts me at odds with the culture, and without studying and personally analyzing the Scriptures, how am I going to stand up to that scrutiny? "All Scripture is inspired by God," we read in 2 Timothy 3:16, "and profitable . . . for training in righteousness."

Each person needs to understand the Scriptures as an indi-vidual and not just listen to what a pastor or a priest says. Although I believe that there are fundamental truths in the Bible, the way each person applies them to his life is different. Christ was resurrected. Heaven and hell are real. These are basic points of the faith, but Christians come up with many cultural absolutes based on assumptions and conclusions that aren't accurate and can't be supported by what is written in the Word of God.

For example, the whole Old Testament is full of stories of people messing up again and again and God having mercy and grace on them until it gets to a certain point that He says, "I've got to teach you what you're doing wrong. I've got to punish you." The idea of a punishing God is very hard for people to accept. But as a believer in the Word, I not only have to accept those truths and deal with them, but I also have to be ready with an answer when others confront me with their doubts and disbelief.

Because God has made us each unique, we understand Him in different ways. For one person a passage in the Bible can be a stumbling block. For another person it can be a revelation. Each person has to decide for himself, which doesn't mean that I'm throwing out the validity of teachers and preachers. But it's important to remember that they're human, like the rest of us.

Setting an Example

Human beings are always going to let each other down, and for that reason I think the church, which sometimes elevates its leaders above where they belong, has a lot to answer for. There are all kinds of negative aftereffects of poor leadership. All of us have seen those zany TV shows and the people with pink and purple hair, begging for money in the name of Jesus. I don't think that's something Christ really appreciates. He was a man of the people, accessible to prostitutes and beggars and people with leprosy. Isaiah 53:3 describes Him as "a man of sorrows and acquainted with grief." I don't find that quality in many church leaders these days, and although I don't want to be judgmental, I can't help but cringe when I see that stuff on TV. If that's the reaction of a Christian, what is a nonbeliever going to think?

Ultimately we have to look to Jesus as our example in everything. He reached out to people from every walk of life, hung with them and helped them and healed them. There's a reason He was crucified. People wanted to shut Him up. He wasn't a safe individual. And in that, He set an example for us to follow.

> *"I believe in the angelic race. And I believe there are fallen angels. I believe that spiritual warfare goes on all around us and that we can discover its reality through signs and symbols of the time."*

Each day I try the best I can to live by that example, to look beyond the circumstances to the eternal significance of life, to grasp the spiritual in everything. I love music and art that lead me to lofty ideals, the truths that aren't right in front of our eyes. I think that if I hadn't become a Christian, I would definitely have been into some mystical religion because it's ludicrous to live in this world without seeing that there's another plane of existence all around us.

I believe in the angelic race. And I believe there are fallen angels. I believe that spiritual warfare goes on all around us and that we can discover its reality through signs and symbols of the time. I'm trying to serve my term as a foot soldier in that battle, and I think that God has put unique weapons at my disposal.

And if it's true for me, then it's true for you. Each person has a job to do, and my job is to intrigue people with words and music and get them to look around corners to see the truth that's in plain sight. Is there a God? Is there a devil? Do I have a responsibility to my Creator? Are there consequences to what I do? These questions can open up the boxes that trap too many of us.

I like to partake fully in the adventure of life, but at the same time I try to recognize my limitations in the adventure. As surely as God gave us strengths, He gave us weaknesses, and it's up to us to live within the guidelines He has established.

Knowing the guidelines requires a very personal interaction between each individual and God. For instance, I've been accused of promoting the drinking of alcohol. But Christ's first miracle was making good wine at a wedding party, and I don't think He had anything particular against alcohol, except that we should never allow ourselves to be ruled by alcohol or anything else other than the law of God. I use drinking as an example because the issue of whether to abstain is one of the most obvious stumbling blocks for many people. I think the same thing would be true of eating too much food or watching too much TV.

Sex, Drugs, and Rock and Roll

Maybe you want to stop me right there. Am I advocating drug use or worse? No, but I have to be honest. I had my share of experiences in college, and I didn't stop because I was afraid of getting busted for doing things I knew were wrong. I stopped because drugs weren't helping me further my spiritual or artistic goals. They slowed me down and made me dull. I respect the authority of man's law, but the real issue is God's law. Are you doing something that is bringing you closer to Him or taking you farther away?

God wants us to consider how our actions affect others. Scripture says to avoid the appearance of evil, and we are not to eat meat in front of a brother who is a vegetarian just to prove we're free. (You can read about it in 1 Corinthians 8.) The point is even more critical for a person in my position. I have to be careful about what I do in public and make sure that the exercise of my freedom isn't an affront to others. I don't think it's wrong to have a beer. But maybe somebody else does, somebody whose father was an alcoholic and beat him while under the influence.

We've got to be accountable for our actions, before God and to each other. He created wine and food and television, and He left it up to us to exercise our free will when it comes to things that may be harmful or excessive in our lives. Man has taken God's creation and perverted it to his own ends. Our role as believers is to assist in the redemption of that creation.

There's probably no more important act of redemption than in the area of sex. I strongly believe that having sex before marriage is an abuse of something that God meant for good and created for our pleasure. Sex is a supernatural bonding between a husband and a wife. The fact that my wife was a virgin when we were married allowed her to experience sexuality the way God intended it. I only wish that the same had been true for me.

Man has perverted a good thing and reduced it to a mere physical act. There's no beauty, awe, or wonder in sex just for the sake of sex. In fact, a heavy emotional and spiritual toll comes with sharing a bed with someone who seems appealing. Casual sex just confuses what the body and spirit truly want and need. It's no wonder that so many people in my line of work—musicians and performers—usually end up self-destructing. When someone is taking as many drugs as he can and drinking as much as he can and having sex with as many people as he can, it's inevitable that he is going to crash when he comes off the high. It's his body's way of telling him that it isn't made for that kind of abuse. There's such a thing as too much freedom.

We live under a natural law established by God. Because we're born instinctively knowing that law, we understand inherently what's good and evil. And if we ignore that instinct, we pay the price *every time*.

Personally I'd like to stick around for a long time and have the chance to see how the story of my generation turns out. I even like to believe that I might have a small part to play in the outcome. I'm not trying to win everyone over, but I know that people who live their lives not caring about the truth are in more trouble than people who ask questions and express their doubts and look for answers. They are trying to find out who they are, regardless of how far that puts them outside the mainstream. These seekers are going to accept the truth more quickly than the people who are afraid to be honest with themselves and allow themselves to become more and more dishonest as time goes by. They're sinking into a hole, and when they're thrown the line of truth, they'd rather cower and hide deeper in the hole than grab hold of a way out.

I also believe that the church should be holding out that lifeline. It saddens me that some leaders in the church are nothing more than politicians who want to impress the masses and gather a following. If they were sincere about their ministries, they wouldn't worry so much about making everybody happy or trying to make truth acceptable to everyone. Searching people need to know the reality of Jesus Christ, but they also need to know that Christianity is a challenge and that they aren't going to meet that challenge without God's mercy and their own surrender. As Christians, we're bound to fall on our faces trying on our own to make it work for us. God created the Ten Commandments knowing full well that we wouldn't be able to live them out, that we'd have to turn to Him for the strength to do His will.

Unlimited Grace

I'm not a teacher, and I'm not especially intellectual. But I can tell you what I feel in my heart, and I can be up front about the experiences of my life. That's the best way I know to point people to the truth. I believe I can help others when I explain how I'm trying to realize my part in God's design. Generally the world is a pretty disillusioned place.

As I learn more about God's grace and God's characteristics, I aspire to be able to provide some answers through my music to the questions that we have about our destinies.

My goal is to be a great artist and a great Christian, yet I realize that I'm only human and I struggle as everyone else does. I just want people to extract some hope, some peace, and some truth from my music and from the example of my life.

> "I just want people to extract some hope, some peace, and some truth from my music and from the example of my life."

God has an unlimited amount of grace for each of us, but I don't think we fully understand that. I grew up in a legalistic church, and the message I heard was all about God punishing us when we did something wrong. There was no counterbalance of mercy. However, Jesus said, "Be merciful, just as your Father is merciful" (Luke 6:36). Emphasizing only one aspect of God without letting others be revealed cheapens our faith.

Hearing about God's grace gets me excited, and I want to spread the word. That's one thing I'm trying to get across in my music and in the pages of this book. I hope that, by the end of it, I'll be a person you can relate to. But more important, I hope you can see that God works in my life in the same way that He works in yours. I hope you'll be encouraged to go for the thing that is truest in yourself. I hope you'll realize that God designed you to be unique and that your uniqueness has a purpose in His plan. And I'm convinced that if each of us could realize that purpose, we could shake the world.

To become those things, we have to get a glimpse of the big picture. If we think about the universe and the way everything interlocks, it takes a whole lot more faith *not* to believe in God than it does to accept His intelligent handiwork in creation. I have a few friends who are atheists, and although I can understand their position, it's not very well thought out. They haven't investigated deeply enough, gone below the surface, or done their homework. That's what we have to do if we're going to make any difference in this life. But it's not easy. And sometimes it can be very lonely.

I've never felt that I belonged to any interest group or common community. I've always been an outsider, and sometimes I can draw strength from remembering that. I've enjoyed being a misfit and living on the fringe with other people who aren't like everyone else. But I would be remiss if I didn't admit that I've gained my greatest strength from being accepted by the One who created me.

Realizing how much God loves us as individuals is the first step in understanding who we are and what we're created to be. And it's always so much more than we can imagine. Too many of us get caught up in co-opting others' identities and ideas, trying to fit in as opposed to standing out. We follow the marching orders of the powers that be in the entertainment industry and the fashion industry and the political industry— and the list goes on and on. They're the ones who teach us to do what everybody else does because then we're easier to manipulate. We become faceless, mindless consumers. Only when we get outside those boxes and try something different does life become truly interesting, and we discover the joy of being ourselves.

The Singer and the Song

That brings me back to where I started. The *me* I want to be has a lot to do with the songs I want to sing. Recently I had the chance of a lifetime—to record my first solo album after being part of dc Talk for so long. As you might well imagine, I put everything I had, heart and soul, into that album. And if someone asked me to explain what I did and why, more than likely I would say—you guessed it—"The song says it all."

In truth, there's more to say about me being me and you being you than I could sum up on a CD in a little more than an hour. So I'm trying something new, something that leaves the music whole, open to interpretation and the personal spin that can make songs so meaningful, but at the same time I hope that I offer some insight and illustration, context and commentary on the lifetime of *being* that's gone into my music.

I've named each chapter of this book after a song on my new album to provide a closer look not just at the song, but at the singer, my life story, and the lessons and insights I want to pass along.

You can listen and read, or read and listen, or do one or the other. This book and the CD are meant as much to stand on their own as they are to be complementary. One expresses itself in words on a page, the other in digitally coded audio signals, because what I've discovered in this strange multimedia experiment is that the inspiration and impetus for my music simultaneously reach far back into the past and far forward into the future. There *is* a story behind these songs, a point of view and the sum total of a lot of hard-won experience.

It's a story about the power and responsibility that God has given each one of us to *be* who we are to the best of our ability. It's a subject each of us could write a book about. This one just happens to be mine.

There may come a time when you'll have an opportunity to tell your life story and pass along the wisdom and experience you gathered. When that time comes, the book of your life will be as unique as you are. God made only one of each of us. It's up to us to make the most of our individuality.

Track One

RETURN OF THE SINGER

I'm coming out like a .45
Spinning like a Wurlitzer on overdrive
Feeling like electro glide
Touch down satellite, feel all right
Tonight, return of love
Return, return of the singer

Twist me up and watch me burn
Just like a falling star about to burst
Center down and outward thrust
The curtain's up, baby, it's all or bust
Tonight, return all the love you get
Return, return of the singer

It's tailor made and it's heaven sent
Just think about the time we've spent
The way we moved, the words we spent
If nothing else a testament
Oh my love, oh my baby
No one else can make me crazy like you, like you

'Cause we're all about to move on
No one here without a song
Pilfering the planet's blood
Been making up the moment from after the flood
Tonight, return of love
Return, return of the singer

I'll tell you how it's gonna be
We're gonna make some history
A microphone, the truth we need
No joke, no trend, no fad of the week
Hordes of angels, sing as one
You know my heart has come undone again, again

Return, return of love
Return, return of the singer
Return of all the love you get
Return, return of the singer

RETURN OF THE SINGER

The first cut of an album is like the first chapter of a book: it sets the tone, creates the mood, and states the purpose. In the case of my opening song, I think it also tells a lot about who I am and what I'm trying to say with my music.

On "Return of the Singer" I wanted to make a statement about how I felt finally being able to make a solo album. It's almost as if I had taken a break from dc Talk and had "returned" as a new character. I guess I'll always be known as the singer in dc Talk, but my hope is that this record lets people see more sides to me than only that role. I hope they'll also see that I'm a lyricist and a melody maker, that I'm a person with several diverse elements.

The song starts out with a tongue-in-cheek attitude as if I'm bragging about being a star, being infallible and feeling like a god because of the way audiences respond to me. I'm having a little fun with the whole image factory of rock music, but it is true that when I do a show, I want people to get their money's worth. I want to inspire others, not just to go out and buy my record, but to write their thoughts down and make their own music.

It's a song that announces in no uncertain terms that I've arrived with a vengeance, and that I'm out to prove that I'm more than just one-third of dc Talk. But as much as it may seem that I'm copping an attitude, the reality is, I aim to please, and I'm ready to put on a fantastic show.

The song says, "Hordes of angels, sing as one / You know my heart has come undone," which is a reflection of the great moments I've had with dc Talk. So many nights, especially on the *Jesus Freak* tour, there was an amazing presence of the Spirit when we hit the stage. We felt God at some of those shows, and it was a majestic experience every time, like singing before the throne of the Almighty. Knowing that God is listening when I sing is an overwhelming concept, and some of that awe and wonder went into this song too.

> "I love rock and roll music, and I love inviting my friends along to the party we're having on the stage."

In essence, every song I sing is for the Creator, a way of saying thank You for giving us the gift of music and for allowing this moment to happen.

I have a mighty concept of God, and because I feel so loved, I want to give it all back to Him. That's where music comes from, and when I'm onstage and all the people are with me, praising their Creator, well, that's the awesome thing about Christian music and what sets it apart from other musical experiences. It's the closest thing I can imagine to those heavenly creatures singing of God's glory, described in Revelation 4:8. The audience may be there to praise us—and that can be a flattering feeling—but it gets really old, especially compared to people actually celebrating the Creator and getting spiritual inspiration from my music.

Of course, a person can get lost in that, too, and I think some Christian entertainers get confused by thinking that they're God's emissaries or that He has empowered them with special gifts, beyond those of anyone else. There's a danger to thinking like that because God doesn't need any of us to help Him out. Some artists take the viewpoint that God needs their music out there to evangelize the world. They need to recognize that we have the privilege of serving Him, not the other way around.

I try to keep it simple. I love rock and roll music, and I love inviting my friends along to the party we're having on the stage. If God is blessed by that, great! I believe He really was blessed by what was happening with dc Talk around the time of albums such as *Free at Last, Jesus Freak,* and *Supernatural.* Those records in particular moved people in a special way, and I've gotten thousands of letters telling me that in a dark time, our music really turned things around for people and helped them get through it because of what we were saying and because of the ideas and the passion behind the music.

Look, I wouldn't be honest if I said I wasn't affected by the adulation of the crowd. But I'm also being honest when I say I've gotten past the screams and hysteria by now. What excites me is seeing an audience lifted up and being brought nearer to God through music. Nothing comes close to that experience. I know my music is more subtle, not nearly as straight ahead a Christian message as what dc Talk offers, and I'm cool with that. I want it to have a universal appeal. I want a Buddhist to be able to come to my show and have just as good a time as a Christian does.

A song is more than the words in the lyrics, no matter how meaningful they might be to the person who wrote them. The music has always come first with me, and I know for a fact that the impact of any song is carried, first and foremost, by the elements of rhythm, tempo, and melody. I think it's also true that music has a meaning, with or without words. That is why, if you want to know what an artist is saying in a song, you need to know how it came together in the first place.

East Meets West

"Return of the Singer" was written in a Los Angeles hotel room with a very simple idea in mind. Because it was to be the introductory song on the record, it was key that it could also be performed as a piece of live music. Live playing is what music is all about to me. I really understand a piece I've written when I perform it again and again, and I start seeing what it can do for people and how they are taking it in. The song started with a very basic idea of a dance rhythm. I brought a friend of mine, a computer programmer, over to the hotel and told him I wanted a European dance track, but with a rock edge to it. We designed it from the beginning to be played live.

When we got into the studio to record it, one of the first jobs of the producer was what I call "debugging." I was such a huge fan of groups like the Beatles, Queen, and Roxy Music, and they had such a significant musical influence on me, that we had to debug the sound of those elements. I wanted my record to be uniquely my own, and that process began right there in the studio.

We all worked very hard on the song arrangement, the part of the puzzle that provides the right combination of instruments to create a tone and a mood. We used strings and some effects that sounded like a sitar because I wanted a definite Eastern influence. I've always been interested in that realm, from the dabbling of George Harrison to the classical Indian sounds of Ravi Shankar. It's just got that mystical and ancient spiritual feel to it. The Western world is intriguing, but there's more beyond what we're familiar with, and the world of the East fascinates me.

The strong appeal of Eastern culture and art to me had puzzled me until I learned more about my heritage. If it's true that we inherit certain traits or characteristics from our parents, then that explains a lot, at least in my case. You see, I was adopted as a baby. Years later, when I finally met my birth parents, I understood more about who I was and what I gravitated to, most especially music. My biological father, who has a very

Irish-sounding name, is an all-around musician, a bassist and guitarist and drummer who sings. He played in several bands in the 1960s, which was a time when a generation was making up its own rules. He was a hippie. He lived in a commune on

Kevin as a baby

the fringes of society, totally committed to the rock and roll lifestyle. He was into yoga and for a while owned a yoga studio where he taught hatha yoga; he was a real free spirit who was drawn to Zen Buddhism. In his life, he carries parts of other religions that are valuable to his faith. He's a very spiritual man, but more in the Eastern sense of that term.

I try not to judge anyone for what he believes, but at the same time I'm not afraid to let others know where I'm coming from. I made the decision to ask Christ to come into my life at the age of twelve. I was totally sure of what I was doing. I'd read the Scriptures and knew what they meant for my life. And at such a young age, I regarded that as pretty substantial evidence that God had a future for me. The Bible has many different facets to it, and accepting it is a matter of blind faith for many people. I never had much doubt. Throughout the years, like everyone else, I've drifted and rebelled sometimes, wondering how I became a Christian in the first place. But I knew the truth and I never really parted from it.

Nevertheless, I think that even if I didn't believe in Christ as Savior, I would definitely still be a very spiritual person. That's just the way I was made, even though it's not always easy for me to fit into an organized religious structure. I have come to believe that, although church is an important aspect of any Christian's life, it's still possible to have a vital relationship with God outside the sanctuary walls. Romans 1:20 reminds us that since the creation of the world, God's "invisible attributes, His eternal power and divine nature, have been clearly seen." Just look around you!

Life on the Fringe

I went to Christian schools for the majority of my adolescent years, which sometimes made me feel as if I were in a bubble. I always felt closer to the fringe people and the non-Christian kids. I found the people on the outside more interesting, more easygoing, and not quite so worried about cultural absolutes.

As a result, I did my share of partying—drinking, smoking, and meeting girls. I found myself living on the fringes, too, lying to my adoptive parents and telling them I was hanging out with my Christian school buddies when I was actually meeting up with some friends and heading to a big field outside of town, lighting a bonfire, and just kicking back. I struggled with that lifestyle, but the truth is, I never completely gave in to it. I never said to myself,

> "I went to Christian schools for the majority of my adolescent years, which sometimes made me feel as if I were in a bubble."

"This is what I want to do, and I am going to turn my back on what I have always believed." I wanted to see what the outside world was like because I was tired of being in that bubble. And when I saw what was happening out there, I didn't buy into it. It might have been fun for a short time, but it wasn't nearly as meaningful as my real spiritual heritage.

My adoptive parents were devoted Christians and wonderful people. My dad, Max, was the son of a farmer/factory worker. His was a poor family that had lived in Indiana before moving to Grand Rapids, Michigan, where I was raised. My mother, Elaine, grew up in a very conservative Baptist family: no dancing, no drinking. Their whole notion of partying was going out and having dinner with friends and then coming back to the house and just talking. At the age of four I started singing, and my parents took me all over the place to churches in the area, really encouraging me and my talents.

By the time I was a teenager, I knew that music was what I wanted to do for the rest of my life. While I was primarily singing in churches, I also did a lot of musicals at school. The first time I really tuned into rock and roll was when a neighbor played me *The Game* by Queen. Immediately something hit me. This friend, who was about three years older than I was, went on to introduce me to the Moody Blues, the Beatles, and various other great artists. A cousin gave me my first rock record—John Lennon's *Shaved Fish*—and I remember being impressed by the beautiful melodies and deep lyrics.

Naturally I wanted to start a band and delve deeper into rock and roll. Although my parents never exactly forbade it, they tried their best to steer me in another direction. They weren't lame adults by any means, and they weren't entirely sheltered, either. My dad was a big Elvis fan, and both of them liked country music, but it was obvious to me that they were more than a little disappointed with the path I was heading down. To them, rock and roll represented the unknown. And that was the same mysterious quality that I couldn't seem to get enough of. I had a growing appetite for rock, and I started listening to everything. I remember printing *AC/DC* and *Black Sabbath* and *Judas Priest* on my jean jacket, which in Michigan at that time was the cool thing for teens to do. As much as anything, we did it because it freaked out our parents.

I think my mom and dad always knew that I was going to be in music professionally, but that notion scared them because the profession seemed insecure. My dad was an accountant, and he had put himself through school. My mom was a housewife. Mom and Dad couldn't have children of their own, but they put everything they had into their adopted son. The reality was, they were very loving people, and I had a solid upbringing. My rock and roll rebellion wasn't different from that of any other kid my age, except in one key respect. And to me, that one thing made all the difference in the world.

The Truth Hurts

Right around that time, when I was fifteen, I discovered the circumstances of my birth. My parents had told me as a child that I was adopted, but it didn't really hit me until I was a teenager and I found some papers in my dad's study describing my birth parents. I was going through his paperwork, looking for something in his desk drawer, when I discovered that my biological father was a rock musician.

My first thought was that they had been trying to keep a

big secret from me, something that would explain who I was and what my destiny would be, and I was very angry. The reality was, they were just putting off telling me the details, waiting until I was old enough to handle them, which was definitely *not* at age fifteen.

After the shock wore off, I began thinking of myself as some kind of foundling prince. I started daydreaming

A young Kevin

about the fact that my father could be anybody, even one of the big stars I idolized. After all, the papers said he had an Irish background, and a lot of my favorite musicians were from that part of the world. I found out some other things, too, things I couldn't quite wrap my head around. My dad had other children, all my half brothers and sisters, by different women. He'd met my mother when she was a student and his band was playing a gig in Minneapolis. Those people had obviously lived a far different life from anything I'd experienced, and it all seemed very romantic and cool. I fantasized about what my history might have been if things had turned out differently.

And one aspect of my life that I questioned the most at that time was my belief in Jesus Christ. From the time I was twelve and had that wake-up call, I never had any reason to doubt my Christian assumptions, but all of a sudden I found myself wondering whether I had accepted those ideas only because they were what I'd been taught.

Though church had always been a big part of my family life, I never felt as if I completely fit in. I never got heavily involved in the youth groups and never was able to strongly relate to anybody in my church circle. As a teenager, I felt as if I were living in the shadows with a secret life that my parents didn't know anything about. Yet I struggled with that alienation and never completely gave in to it. "Train up a child in the way he should go," the Bible instructs in Proverbs 22:6. "Even when he is old he will not depart from it."

But if I didn't exactly belong in the church and I didn't exactly belong in the world, where *did* I belong? The music I listened to was like forbidden fruit; tasting it inspired me in ways that few other things could. It was the same with books. I started getting into science fiction and fantasy about that time, and I became a huge fan of Frank Herbert's *Dune* series. J. R. R. Tolkien's *The Lord of the Rings* trilogy left a mark on me, and I loved Conan, the Barbarian. The Dark Ages and Gothic culture were compelling to me, and I was drawn to the darker aspects of literature, such as the stories by Edgar Allan Poe.

"The Quay"

Personally I don't think there's anything wrong with those interests. Life is full of contrasting shades, and we need to have experiences that help us understand the forces that are at work in the world, black and white. At the same time, we need a foundation of truth to help us sort through the influences that shape us, and I know that having a strong connection to God from an early age kept me from going too deeply into the darkness.

> "We need a foundation of truth to help us sort through the influences that shape us."

Honesty has always made an impression on me. A writer or singer who is being honest, even if he isn't coming from a Christian point of view, has real power and integrity. It's what I've tried to reach for in my music. Even as a kid writing poetry, I wanted to say something real—which wasn't always easy, especially since I wasn't exactly sure what *was* real. As far back as grade school, I was writing little short stories, trying for a Shel Silverstein or a Lucy-in-the-Sky-with-Diamonds effect.

When I was in the sixth grade, I wrote a poem called "The Quay" about a mythical creature that lived in trees and spied on people. The idea came directly from the science fiction, fantasy, and rock and roll world I was living in. That was part of how I learned to express myself, using raw material and refining it into something that reflected who I was and what I was thinking and feeling.

Of course, once I knew what I had to say, I had to find someone to listen. That's what being onstage is all about. The opportunity to express myself truly and deeply is a powerful motivating force in my life. In fact, it's a little overpowering at times. I have a strong desire for that validation, a hunger that I have to be careful to keep under control, because in my musical career with dc Talk, I've been pretty spoiled. We developed an audience quickly, and that audience is very loyal to us.

When I'm onstage singing a song and the people are singing it back to me, it's as if I've made a personal, emotional connection. And it really doesn't matter who that other person might be. My hope is that even a hard-core atheist could come to one of our shows and enjoy what's going on. I think even atheists will agree that there is a spiritual yearning inside everyone to understand the blueprint and plan of life. In Romans 8:19, Paul said it this way: "The creation waits eagerly for the revealing of the sons of God."

And that brings me back to "Return of the Singer." I wanted that song to have depth. As much as it's about getting onstage and having a good time, shaking my booty and setting things off, it goes farther than that and exposes a vulnerable part of me. I make mistakes. I'm just like anyone else. I need God to guide me. People might say I've got it made. I'm part of a popular group. We've made hit records. But the truth is, that's not enough. Everyone needs to change and grow. All my favorite artists have been people who constantly changed, tried to better themselves, evolve, and take their art farther.

I honestly have to say that there have been times when I felt that I hit a ceiling with dc Talk. Being in the group wasn't lining up with who I was. I was being loyal to my friends and fans, but not really doing what I needed to do and what I was called to do.

Please don't misunderstand. I'm very proud of dc Talk's music and very proud of what we've done as a group together. But sometimes I've just been playing a character within that group. In the beginning I wanted a chance to sing, to get into the studio and onto the stage. I have a hunger to make my own kind of music, however, and dc Talk doesn't always provide that outlet. I realized I needed to go out and try it on my own, then come back to the group when I'd accomplished that goal.

dc Talkin'

So where does that leave my future with dc Talk? The reality is, I will always have a strong bond, personally, spiritually, and even creatively with my band mates. The way I look at it, we started out as friends and became brothers. We may not see eye to eye on some things, but that doesn't change the fact that we love and respect each other. We've been a very, very close unit for years, living in the same apartment, touring in the same cramped buses, playing together night after night. Simply put, dc Talk has been a big part of my life. The group has afforded me many great opportunities, given me a platform, and led me to meeting my wife. Yet I'm an individual, separate and complete from the band, and I think that everyone has to establish his identity, on his own, without having to depend on labels to explain or define him.

The other guys in the band have always been sympathetic

to my wanting to do projects outside dc Talk. All of us realized about the time that *Jesus Freak* came out that each one had aspirations beyond the band, even if, on occasion, we've had a hard time letting go of the security that being in a hit group represents. We've sold millions of records, and we aren't ready to walk away from that. But we've learned to make room for each other's individuality, which I think is a valuable lesson for anyone, in any walk of life, to learn. The music of dc Talk is an art form, one created by three very distinct and opinionated people. It may be different from my music in that it has more of an evangelical bent, but we've never been just another Christian group, singing feel-good songs.

> "The music of *dc Talk* is an art form, one created by *three* very distinct and opinionated people."

We've tried to be honest and up front about our faith, and as a result, thousands of people have told us that they have received Christ through our shows. I think it's wonderful that we've been able to steer them toward the truth. But they should look to God to set the example. He's the One who saved them, not me. I'm just drawing a picture, which they can look at and see the beauty of God. They've made the choice to respond.

That is what I want to do with my music, which is very different from the dc Talk approach. It's more of a King David style than an apostle Paul style. I want people to know that I have a deep faith, but I sometimes struggle with my faith, and I have the same weaknesses as anyone else. At the end of the day I also have the peace of knowing that God is merciful and He's on my side.

Whether yours is a King David or an apostle Paul style—or some other approach all your own—the strength you will need to achieve the goals He has set before you will come from recognizing what you do best and where you need the support and encouragement of others. Above all, if you remember that God is for you, that He wants you to succeed beyond your wildest dreams, then nothing can stop you.

Above:
Kmax and
Jerry Falwell

Kmax and friend
Christian, posing
at the ranch

Kevin and half brother Satya

Track Two

EXISTENCE

You come into the threshold of another
      starless night of fear
You're running from the demons that
      would drag you down again
Illusions of the world are spinning out
      of time and frame and synchronicity

You're so sad, you're such a sad-eyed girl
You're so sad, in your subplot

Chorus
What is this, what is this, this mess of my existence is
All these politics of life and death and relevance
It's my existence

Another morning it comes running up
    your bedpost with the wind
You face yourself just like you always do,
    time and time again
The mortal coil of image, inner peace,
    and satisfaction

And so you keep it on the down-low
Hiding all the secrets that are down below
And so you keep it on the down-low
Tell me, baby, was it worth it all?

Chorus
Oh just take it all, make it work and make some sense
Just take it all, You're my existence
You're my existence

EXISTENCE

With the song "Existence" I wanted to write something that everybody could relate to. When I started putting down the lyrics and melody, I was thinking about how lots of people I know, some of them close friends, are searching for a deeper meaning to their lives. The song itself pays homage to the person who is searching for truth, peace, and significance. Sometimes that search can get pretty tough, whether or not you're a believer in Jesus.

Initially I wrote it in the first person, but then decided it would be more interesting to take it from another person's point of view, and I chose a female character, a "sad-eyed girl" who is running from the hard things in her life. I had in mind someone living in the fast lane in Los Angeles or New York, a fictional character such as a model or an actress, trying to become somebody, but also avoiding the consequences of her choices and getting involved with people and things that have the potential to destroy her.

I set out to examine the conflicts of a person who wants to find fulfillment and thinks that the way to achieve that goal is to be rich and successful, to try to lay hold of security through material things. There's a point at the end of the song where I've tried to turn the meaning around so that it becomes a cry to God, asking Him to make sense of the character's life, to give her purpose and resolve. We all get wrapped up in our desires, bogged down by the things of the world and giving in to temptation, but I hope that those experiences make us ready to learn and to discover where true wisdom is found.

> "You have to make some serious commitments and sacrifices to become a grounded spiritual person."

People talk as if being a Christian is supposed to solve all the problems in life, as if it's the end of struggling and searching. But in my experience, it's just the beginning. You have to make some serious commitments and sacrifices to become a grounded spiritual person, and in "Existence" I try to be up front about that process. It's about living life honestly, feeling lonely and empty but not giving up. Now that's something worth striving for. Through all your pitfalls and mistakes, you can find joy and rest.

Stating that from a woman's point of view gives the song an extra impact, I think. Women in our society are under more pressure than men to look and act perfectly. It's more important for a woman than for a man to be attractive. But there's

Kmax and his mother on his first Harley-Davidson

another difficult aspect to a woman's position in the culture. It's as if we've forgotten that there is a basic and fundamental difference between the sexes.

It goes back to Genesis, when God made Adam a helpmate out of his own body because He could see that the man needed companionship. But a woman does more than complete a man. Without women we men become isolated and shut off. Women are more open, more in tune with their emotions and with spiritual realities than many men are. It's a powerful source of strength, yet they're not allowed to freely exercise it. Women are told they have to be more like men to succeed in this world.

Fumbling in the Dark

A living example of a godly woman was my adoptive mother. When I was growing up, she showed me a lot of love and gave me self-confidence, but she was also to be feared in the good sense of that word. She was stalwart and strong willed, and from her I learned to have great respect for women. As a consequence, I've been drawn to females for their unique perceptions. I always ask women their opinion when it comes to choices I have to make because I value their point of view. For that reason I've never had a problem getting along with women.

That isn't to say the issue of commitment has been a breeze for me. I've been on the road so much, concentrating on my music, that I've rarely been in a position to spend much time with one person. I had a couple of extended relationships before I joined dc Talk, but I never dated a girl for a long period of time until I met my wife, Alayna. Unfortunately that kind of rootless life doesn't build lasting connections with people, and often left me feeling more lonely and isolated than before.

As I said, I had a couple of sexual encounters before my marriage, and as painful as the consequences were, they taught me that having sex with someone I didn't really love was like fumbling in the dark, trying to satisfy myself and the other person, but with no real attachment. In that context, sex can leave a person feeling quite miserable. All of the activity leading up to that moment can be exciting, but afterward I walked away from the experiences feeling not very good about myself. And I think the women involved felt the same way, even though they never voiced it to me because they probably were afraid of admitting that the experience wasn't what it was supposed to be. Both they and I suffered, and we had a harder time being friends after those encounters because, whether people want to believe it or not, sex creates strong emotional bonds.

God has set forth very clear rules about sex because He knows that in the confines of marriage we've made a commitment and we're more likely to stick by that commitment. "Marriage is to be held in honor among all," we read in Hebrews 13:4, "and the marriage bed is to be undefiled." Emotional and spiritual connections between the man and the woman are vital in a marriage. And sex, when united with those elements, is the ultimate expression of love and commitment.

It brings everything together, and if two people don't have those connections before they have the sexual connection, they have cheated themselves.

Of course, some people would argue that they've had sex with lots of different partners. What they're talking about is just a physical act. It's not really the union of two people; it's more like a sporting event involving sheer athleticism. And that cheapens it.

Many things in this world cheapen sex. For example, when I'm out on the road and girls approach me, succumbing to the temptation would be the easiest thing in the world. Exactly because it's so easy, so available, I've tried to stay clear of it. It's just a meaningless encounter and one that invariably leaves both people feeling empty and used.

> "When I'm out on the road and girls approach me, *succumbing to the temptation* would be the easiest thing in the world."

You may be surprised to find out that these things go on in Christian music. Although these goings-on are definitely not as common as they are in the rock and roll world, you better believe that they exist. The main difference is that the fear of punishment isn't there for people with no connection to God. In the Christian world, sexual activity is punished; it can ruin an artist's life and career. In the secular world, if someone sleeps with a lot of his groupies, he is celebrated. The notoriety is like a pat on the back because he's living the rock and roll lifestyle that everyone expects of him.

But when the artists who really buy into that lie are telling me what a great time they're having, they're doing it with clenched jaws, trying to convince themselves as much as me. The reality is, they are tortured, miserable people who are very insecure. They don't have a sense of who they are because they're trying to live by their own rules, outside the confines of what God has established for the good of humanity. You don't have to be a theologian to figure it out. You can feel it in your spirit, deep down in your bones, when you do something you know is wrong.

Embedded Expectations

God designed life to be a wonderful, beautiful, freeing experience. It's not about a bunch of rules and regulations. But man has had a tendency from the dawn of time to do things his own way. And the more we pervert God's intent for our lives, the emptier our lives become. By the same token, the more we seek to live under His protection, the more full and complete our lives can become.

How do you do that? Prayer helps. So does taking responsibility for yourself. If you put yourself in a compromising position, you're going to be vulnerable. It's up to you to know your weaknesses and compensate for them accordingly. I'm not saying God helps only those who help themselves, but let's face it: if you put your hand in a frying pan, you're going to get burned. You can put your fingers on that hot skillet and pray, "God, please don't let me get burned." But you're going to end up with blisters. I can guarantee it.

It all comes down to expectations and what you want to get out of your life. Do you have high standards, or are you willing to settle for what someone else tries to convince you is worthwhile? No matter who you are, you have one thing in common with everyone else—a search for meaning. We're all seeking something. Those tattooed boys in suburbia with shaved heads listening to Limp Bizkit and Linkin Park are looking for something. A fourteen-year-old girl in a miniskirt with her hair done up and heavy makeup on, heading to the 'N Sync concert—she's looking for something. The older guy living vicariously through memories of his youth—even he's still looking for something.

> "When I look at what the world describes as a desirable lifestyle, I feel like laughing just to keep from crying."

Each person has an innate sense of hope. Either it lies dormant or it's being exercised. Hope can be as simple as the thing that gets us out of bed in the morning and propels us to our day's work. Without hope, without the idea of going for something, we'd just stay under the covers. With hope we have the expectation that something good may happen.

It's an expectation that's embedded deep in everyone, and I think faith goes hand in hand with that expectation too. It keeps us moving forward, accepting that the sky is not going to fall on us, believing that God is out there somewhere, keeping everything under control.

But keeping faith and hope alive and operating in our lives

is a constant battle. There are so many forces and factors in the world vying for our attention and allegiance, trying to telling us how to live and what our lives should mean. When I look at what the world describes as a desirable lifestyle, I feel like laughing just to keep from crying. It's all so empty, so meaningless.

There's so much plain stupidity that comes from a lack of respect for ourselves and other people. We're told that we should do whatever we feel like in a moment without thinking about the consequences. We're told that if we dress just like Britney Spears or one of the Backstreet Boys and hang out at the mall all day and buy all the right CDs and hair gel, then we'll be cool, and being cool means being happy. In the end it all adds up to a life with no goals, no expectation of excellence, nothing to hang on to. We're all being entertained to death, titillated and shocked until we're numb.

Sometimes I get angry because I love fashion and music and movies, but even though I'm in the entertainment business, I know there's more to life than the Next Big Thing. Artists have become marketing tools, spokespeople for whatever products the corporations are pushing. It's all about a prefabricated advertising campaign, trying to turn us into machines whose only purpose is to consume.

Fallen Angels

I don't think I'm being paranoid when I say that I see something behind all this, some controlling force with a dark purpose. That purpose, plain and simple, is to disillusion us, to get us to believe that life is nothing but surviving, getting as much as we can before we check out. We have to ask ourselves where that's coming from. Who's pushing that agenda and selling that program? Is it Satan, or is it just us and our fallen natures?

The only answer I have to offer is that it's obvious we're in a spiritual battle. Mankind is inherently evil. We're born with a sin nature that wars against the spirit, the spiritual self. But does that mean a devil is behind it all, goading us on? I'd have to say yes. Ephesians 6:12 puts it this way: "Our struggle is not against flesh and blood, but against the rulers, against the powers, against the world forces of this darkness, against the spiritual forces of wickedness in the heavenly places."

Scripture refers to the devil time and time again, an angel called Lucifer who rebelled against God and fell from heaven. The problem arises when people, especially Christians, want to pin everything on the devil. Satan was the first rebel, but that spirit of rebellion lives in all of us. We can give in to it, or we can turn away from it. Lucifer works with the choices we make, and he's much more subtle than we give him credit for. He can mask himself in light and distract us with a character such as Marilyn Manson, who, to many Christians, embodies pure evil. But to me, that artist and his act are just bad theater. Pure evil is something more subtle and calculated. It's meant to have a long-range effect. And the scars it leaves are deep and lasting.

The deepest and most lasting reality in human existence is

the love of God. As much as I believe in an active force of evil, I also know that what is meant for evil God means for good. And I can point to the evidence of my life as proof.

Discovering the identity of my birth parents was one of the big turning points in my life. It made me really want to find out where I came from and what my lineage was. Most important, the fact that my father turned out to be a musician solidified my yearning in that same direction. Nevertheless, I was angry with my adoptive parents for withholding my history from me. We had a couple of very impassioned conversations, and I ended up in my room feeling sorry for myself and probably playing my rock and roll records really loud.

I think at the time they felt they probably should have told me the facts earlier, but the truth was, they didn't do anything wrong. It was their judgment call, and it was up to me to get over my feelings. As much as anything, they were trying to protect me, which was what they'd done from the moment they'd brought me home. If they were a bit overprotective and a bit conservative, they were only acting out of love for me, and they were motivated by wanting the best for me in everything. I've never really held it against them because it wasn't a vindictive act.

Eventually I did get over being bitter, but I began to realize that I really wanted to go out and find my birth parents. I had romanticized them in my mind, building them up into something bigger and more fantastic than they could ever be in real life. I had visions of my father being Van Morrison or somebody equally famous. I wondered whether I was Bob Dylan's illegitimate kid. I was so into rock and roll that I half expected to turn out to be rock and roll royalty. Why not?

Meeting Mom and Dad

When I finally got up the courage, I went to the agency that handled my adoption in Grand Rapids, Michigan. A person on the staff found my mother's address, and I wrote her a letter and she responded. The rule was that both parties had to agree to meet, with the agency as the middleman, to protect the clients.

Kevin and his birth mother

A lot went through my mind when I got word that she wanted to get together. I think by then I realized the chances were that I wasn't related to Van Morrison or Bob Dylan or Rod Stewart, and as a result, I didn't have a lot of childish illusions that would have set me up for disappointment.

Coming face-to-face with my birth mother was a very emotional experience. She arrived at my house completely by surprise and turned out to be a very outgoing, gregarious, and lively woman. What struck me immediately was how much we looked alike: blond with blue eyes, and very similar facial features. It was amazing to sit across from her, talking to her and recognizing some of my own expressions and characteristics in her face.

My birth mother eventually set out to find my birth father. She had no idea where he was living, and she hadn't been in contact with him in years. But she did some detective work, found his phone number, and gave it to me. After I called him, he came for a visit.

People who are close to me know that I'm not an extremely emotional person. For example, I don't cry a lot. If I had to guess why, I'd say that the experience of adoption and the doubt it created about my real identity hardened me a little. I think I might have had some subconscious resentment toward my birth parents, and I had no way to resolve my feelings.

Why did they give me up? It was a question that lingered in the back of my mind for years, but finally meeting them went a long way toward answering it. They weren't bad people. They had just made some bad choices. She was nineteen;

he was twenty. She was a college student, and he was in a rock band. They met at one of his shows, dated for six months, and she got pregnant. Her parents didn't want him around, even after he told them he wanted to stay and take responsibility. In the end she gave me up for adoption. It would have been easier for her to abort me because she was in school at the time and had to drop out and go to a home for unwed mothers.

"I'm a poster child for the pro-life cause."

I'm a poster child for the pro-life cause, and I give her a lot of props for what she did. Giving me away wasn't easy, either, but she knew she couldn't provide me with what I needed. I would have been raised by a single mother, which doesn't offer a whole lot of security in a boy's life. My birth mom was a good woman, trying to do the right thing.

That brings me back to my belief that God can and does turn bad situations around. He definitely had a plan for me and put me with my adoptive parents, who provided me with incredible examples of love and nurturing. I'm so different from both of them, more like my birth parents in many ways, but I can see the qualities that they have helped me to develop to compensate for some of my weaknesses. They made me stronger, taught me things that I would have never known otherwise, such as the value of being responsible and logical. My natural tendency is the exact opposite—to be spontaneous and irresponsible, much like my birth parents. I'm convinced I would have turned out to be an artist, no matter what, but my upbringing taught me the value of discipline and working toward my goals. Somehow, through all the trauma and changes, God achieved a wonderful balance in my life.

The saga of my personal journey to discovering myself, who I was and where I came from, may sound dramatic and even romantic, but in reality all of us have to confront those same questions about ourselves, and a lot depends on the answers we find. The point is, we've got to keep asking and keep looking; we must stay focused on the truth about ourselves and the destiny God has appointed for us. Anything less than that is selling ourselves and Him short.

Track
Three

BE

All in all we're fading
Like a soul lost in the wilderness
We're cold and we're cut off from it
Not knowing where it's gonna end

There's a star in Bethlehem, it's calling you
It's a memory of One who made it

Be, be yourself
There's no one who does it quite like you
Be no one else
'Cause if you don't, then who is going to?
You're a tribute to the best of us

We follow everybody else

Not knowing what we're made for
The mecca of the insecure
The sign and mark of the popular
There's a new face on the television
It's a new host with the same derision

Be, be yourself
Don't let the losers tell you what to do
Be no one else
'Cause if you don't, then who is going to?

And the time is now
No reason to look back
Just like an infant born
You've got to catch your breath
And I'm learning, Father
Yes, and I'm going farther

Be, be yourself
There's no one here who does it quite like you
Be no one else
'Cause if you don't, then who is going to?

Light the path you're supposed to see
Just like the salt that filters through the need
Like the star that's falling from the sky
Just like the apple of your Daddy's eye

Written by Kevin Max and Erick Cole. © 2001 Blind Thief Publishing (BMI)
(admin. by EMI CMP) / Sad Astronaught Music (BMI).

"Be" is one of the few songs I've written in which the lyric came to me before the melody. I was very serious about the shape of the song and what I wanted to say with it. It needed to be an anthem, an answer for the dilemma I'd posed in "Existence."

Everyone searches for the meaning and purpose of life. When you find that meaning and realize what your purpose is, you are free to *be* who you are meant to be. You can be yourself instead of a walking corpse, and you can attain an inner strength in your life, transfused with spiritual meaning.

The approach of the song was first to paint a picture of where the world is heading. There is a parallel to the children of Israel walking in the desert, not knowing where they were going, just wandering and wondering if there really was a destination or a destiny.

Then the message changes. The words say, "There's a star

in Bethlehem, it's calling you / It's a memory of One who made it." What I mean is that Jesus was the first One who actually became self-realized. He knew His worth and His mission and the meaning of His life. And He did something about it. "You're a tribute to the best of us" means He was the ultimate example.

> "The search for the true meaning of our lives is a universal goal. So is knowing that we're created for something bigger and better than what people try to tell us to be."

But I also wanted the song to have a more universal scope, even for people outside the Christian experience. We must realize that being ourselves and being who we're meant to be under God's design is so much more powerful than what other people want us to be. And what we're really looking for is exactly what our culture is trying to keep hidden from us. TV won't give us the answers. Movies won't give us the answers. Politicians won't give us the answers. Schoolteachers won't give us the answers. We have to dig deep within ourselves to find out who we're meant to be.

It was really important to me for the song to be honest about the fact that, without a guidebook, without a blueprint, the search is hopeless. That blueprint, of course, is the Scriptures, the only real instruction manual for our lives. The famous passage in Hebrews 4:12 puts it this way: "The word of God is living and active and sharper than any two-edged sword, and piercing as far as the division of soul and spirit, of both joints and marrow, and able to judge the thoughts and intentions of the heart."

The search for the true meaning of our lives is a universal goal. So is knowing that we're created for something bigger and better than what people try to tell us to be. Maybe I'm on a soapbox, but I don't care. There is no more room for counterfeit people and a world of co-opted lives. That's why I hope "Be" can have meaning to somebody who's outside the Christian faith.

We've got to reject this idea that all we can do is just get by, do only what's expected. When I look at the lives of men like William Blake and Albert Einstein and Franz Liszt, people who went farther than most of us can dream, I see people who

Kmax and the in-laws

were truly self-realized. They understood themselves and challenged themselves and wanted to be the best that they could be. They had a fully developed worldview.

To realize yourself is to be yourself. But that realization comes through the process of being humble before God. You have to understand your inadequacies before you can know your true potential. You have to recognize that you're flesh and blood and be able to see your shortcomings and limitations before you fully comprehend your talents and abilities. If you don't know your weaknesses, the enemy can take advantage of them.

Fault Lines

I've learned that from experience. I'd have to say my major weakness is being irresponsible and having a hard time getting on and sticking with a program. I'm too spontaneous, which in some situations can be a strength, but there has to be some moderation, some self-control, or I end up hurting myself and others. Sometimes I speak before I think. Sometimes I stay up until four in the morning when I know I have to be somewhere at eight the next day.

That has been the way I live my life. I'm impassioned by things that I experience, and that inspires me to write and sing and try to express myself. It's part of being an artist, but so is being disciplined, which is where I'm weak. To overcome that weakness, I have to realize that it exists. Then I work twice as hard at being disciplined. And maybe one day I won't have that problem anymore.

If we truly know ourselves and are self-aware, we can conquer our weaknesses, although some problems might be easier to overcome than others. For example, I like to spend money. I see something nice and I want to buy it. It doesn't make a difference whether it costs $10 or $1,000. So I have to discipline myself, realize that weakness, and try to control my impulses, even if it means throwing out my credit cards or living within a budget.

We have to cultivate spiritual disciplines. We need to spend time with God, and I have established a daily routine to do just that. I get in a private place to talk with and listen to my Creator. I tell Him anything and everything. Sometimes it's just mumbling. Sometimes it's just sitting there. And sometimes I wake up and get a phone call and run off to get a coffee and miss it altogether.

The main thing is to try. Ultimately it's not about the routines and rituals I develop. It's about the intent of my heart and how close I'm walking with God. I can be anywhere and pray to Him or ask His advice or call out for help.

But whenever possible, I try to set aside quality time to study the Scriptures. I have to work at keeping focused on that study. Since I've grown up around the Bible, it sometimes doesn't have the allure for me that it once had. That's when I have to try even harder. I know it helps me become a better person, live a better life, and learn to know the will of God. So I try not to approach Bible study as a duty. To me, that kills the spirit that gives the Bible life in the first place.

These days, I'm in a fellowship with believers, and we get

together at least once, maybe twice a week just to talk and pray. It's too easy for me to become an island unto myself, and when I'm isolated, I cut myself off from the very things that can make me stronger. I need to be with like-minded people who can also

"There's *more to life than what they're trying to* sell you."

challenge me, and when I am, I find myself striving to be the best I can be. If I'm sitting at home all day, watching TV on the couch, or even if I'm alone reading the Bible all day, I'm not able to act on what I know is true. God created us to learn from each other as much as to help each other.

The alternative is to leave ourselves open to influences that can overwhelm and undermine our sense of identity. Without being accountable to each other, we can become victims of the forces that are trying to turn us into cookie-cutter versions of some image that's been created out of fantasy and delusion. Too many people are ready to buy into the marketing of a mass concept of conformity that's being fed to us through the media. I don't think people are stupid, but I think too many are lazy. We'd rather be told how to think and act than figure it out for ourselves.

All it takes is one individual to stand up and say, "It doesn't matter whether you look as good as the supermodel on the cover of *Elle* magazine. It doesn't matter that you're not a rock star." There's more to life than what they're trying to sell you. Depth and substance and work can give you long-term fulfillment and relationships that are meaningful. God has created each person as an individual with a unique bundle of skills and talents and abilities and even weaknesses.

Cheap Grace

I see it all the time in the business I'm in. Record companies won't sign talented acts because they're afraid of taking a risk. But they'll sign someone with a homogenized version of the same prepackaged sound that just sold the last five million records, with the same cheesy hook that everybody can mindlessly sing along to.

That's why I wanted to write the song "Be." My prayer for humanity is that we can live life to its fullest and not have somebody else doing it for us. We can be excellent. We can be better than what's expected. And what's expected these days is at an all-time low. I've done a lot of traveling, and I've seen a lot of different cultures and tried my best to understand the enterprise of man. I've come to believe that America and the West have missed out on a lot. We eat fast food. Everything is at our fingertips. We're in a car all day long, from the drive-in burger joint to the drive-in bank teller and eventually to the drive-in mortuary. We don't experience life because we're always in such a hurry to get to the next place and reach the next moment. Our lives are about two things: seeking pleasure and avoiding pain.

But Christ says in the Scriptures that to believe in Him, we'll have to suffer. Part of life, a significant part of life, comes through pain and the rejection of easy pleasures. It's a narrow path we're called to walk, not the wide, easy access on-ramp. But there are a beauty and a depth in giving things up, sacrificing our desires, and refusing to do what everybody else is doing. In the process, we discover the desire that God has given us, the desire that leads us to discovering who we are and who we're meant to be.

> "Part of life, an important part of life, comes through pain and the rejection of easy pleasures."

It's not a popular idea, but trying to be true to who I am has made me a better person and more at peace with myself. When I'm chasing the wind and I'm caught up in my vanity, it's hard to look at myself in the mirror and see who I really am. But at the end of the day, I get better and better at evaluating the face that's looking back at me. Yeah, I've messed up. Yeah, I should have done this. Yeah, I should have said that. And that's exactly the time when I get on my knees and I ask the Lord to forgive me and help me figure it out better for tomorrow. When that happens, a burden, a weight, is taken off. Sure, I have to live with the consequences. But as I said before, God is incredibly generous when it comes to second chances.

Sooner or later, we've got to let Him do the work of humility in our hearts and minds. We've got to let the Spirit bring us low so that we can be lifted up again, renewed and transformed and strengthened to fight another day. People are always telling me how lucky I am to be in a million-selling group, singing for a living and touring the world in front of sold-out crowds. But dc Talk has been a crucible for God's work in the lives of all three of us, just as much as any trial or triumph you might have gone through that's made you a better person in the long run. When I think back on where we came from and how far we've gone, I'm filled with gratitude and humility. God is certainly not finished with me or Toby or Mike, but He has already taken us a long way—and it has been a fantastic ride.

Looking Back on Liberty

It was a ride that began when my parents started prodding me to go to college. The one they picked was Liberty College in Lynchburg, Virginia. It was an unspoken assumption, which was very typical of my parents, saying to me that if I wanted to pursue my education, they thought this school would be a good choice for me. I guess they were like most other moms and dads, manipulative but not overtly so. On the other hand, if I had announced that I wanted to go to the University of Michigan or NYU or wherever, they probably would have let me.

Their reason for wanting to send me to a Christian school wasn't that they felt I was going to get crazy and party the whole time at some other campus. They had given me a religious upbringing, and it just seemed that my higher education would make more sense at a place like Liberty. As a kid, I'd actually wanted to go to a public school, and I'd struggled with the cultural isolation that comes with Christian schooling—that bubble I was talking about.

What clinched my decision to go to Liberty was that a girlfriend of mine, who was enrolled there, told me about a band that had formed and was looking for a singer. That tugged at me; the idea of Christians playing rock and roll seemed very cool. At the time I didn't know much about Christian rock music. I didn't have any preconceptions, good or bad. I'd never heard of Larry Norman or Randy Stonehill or any of those early Christian rock pioneers, and I was barely aware of artists like Michael W. Smith and Sandi Patty. I knew about Petra. They came through Grand Rapids once, and I'd gone to see their show because I was curious about how they would handle Christian themes and concepts through their music. I thought they did a pretty good job, and I could see they were trying to pioneer a new musical approach.

Suffice it to say, the idea of being in a rock and roll band with other Christians was an appealing one for me. Being in *any* band was appealing. I'd never really gone the garage band route in high school because there were never enough musicians around to put something like that together. I had sung in the choirs and was playing and writing music, but I was pretty much all dressed up with nowhere to go.

Some of my first tunes were pretty interesting in that, even then, I was trying to fit a lot of content into the words. I remember the first song I wrote, called "Competition for Ambition," when I was about sixteen; the lyrics described two guys fighting over a girl. I knew basic chords on the piano, so I would write out the tune, then accompany myself and record

Camera shy

it on a tape recorder, play it back, and listen to it. I think I was in love with the sound of my own voice.

But that's as far as it went. I never had the right connections to make music happen in high school. By the time I got to Liberty, I was ready to give it everything I had. I ended up landing the singing job with a group I had heard about. It went by the really terrible name of the Connection Band. I wanted to change it to Justice for All, which wasn't a whole lot better, but in reality I didn't care what we were called. I was just happy to be singing and writing tunes. We did some early demos, and one of my first contributions to the group was a song called "The Eternal Flame," which was inspired by the shrine for John F. Kennedy.

We did a song written by the drummer called "He's My Best Friend," a goofy jazz thing about God, which I thought was pretty lame. But he was the one who started the group, and he called the shots, which meant that I had to run all my material past him. I guess he recognized that I could write lyrics because he gave that job over to me and eventually let me take the band in more of a rock and roll direction.

Armanis in the Closet

One of the Connection Band's first gigs in which I participated was a Halloween party on campus, and I got myself in full costume for the occasion. I put some shellac foam gunk in my hair that made it all spiky with gold sparkles, used heavy eyeliner, and wore a Dracula cape. Our first number was "Sunday Bloody Sunday" by U2, and then we did a Police song and a Rod Stewart cover and one by the Faces, I think. That was when the dean of men called us over to the side of the stage and forbade us to play on the campus anymore because we were doing "worldly" music.

We didn't let that slow us down a bit. We took our act on the road, playing around the area and picking up gigs at other odd places such as roller skating rinks and private parties. I started hanging around with some of the local fringe element, just as I had done in high school. Meanwhile, the drummer booked us at a nearby theme park, which turned out to be owned and operated by Jim Bakker and the PTL Club.

Bakker was actually present at our audition. We made sure to play nothing but Christian music, and we got the gig. At the time I had no idea who Jim Bakker was, and I didn't know anything about PTL. My family never watched Christian television, aside from flipping through the channels, but I could tell by the way everyone treated him that the dude was famous.

We weren't there more than two weeks, playing to one hundred or two hundred people a day sitting in their beach chairs at the water park, when the headlines hit, and the whole place was immediately shut down. Somehow we were recruited to help move out the Bakkers' personal belongings after they'd been evicted from the premises. I'll never forget going to their penthouse apartment, packing up all their stuff, and taking it to where it was being auctioned to pay for all the debts they'd run up. One of my most vivid memories is of walking into Jim's huge bedroom closet and picking up dozens and dozens of suits in plastic bags that had never been opened. There was one Armani after another with the tags still hanging on them.

It was an amazing education in the power of the media and the ability of people to get rich off the faith and hopes of others. I do believe that Jim Bakker really started out with a good heart, trying to reach people for God. But the whole ministry got twisted by the money and the power and the fame, which proves that Christians are just as vulnerable as anyone else when it comes to the wiles of the world.

In my opinion, Jim Bakker showed what he was made of by

the sincerity of his repentance. Several other evangelists and preachers in the limelight have fallen hard and haven't been repentant about it at all. That, to me, is as big a sin as their original wrongdoing. I mean, how can you really believe in God, then offend Him and not want to repent and ask for forgiveness? If Christians have anything over the world, it's our access to the mercy of God. Without it, we might as well give up right now. Jim Bakker asked for forgiveness from people he had wronged, up front, on TV. That's as much as anyone can ask and no less than anyone has the right to expect.

> "If Christians have anything over the world, it's our access to the mercy of God."

After that experience, the Connection Band broke up, and for a while I forgot about my musical ambitions and even my studies at school. I started spending more and more time with the people I had met outside the closed circle of Liberty College. I started partying pretty intensely and dating one girl after another. I was getting way into my own orbit, far beyond the gravitational pull of Liberty with its dress codes and curfews and rules against going to movies and everything else. I was rebelling completely against the system, but I was doing it in secret as if I didn't really have the courage of my convictions.

From my point of view, the school administrators seemed to be making up the rules as they went along. Over time I think they realized that many of those regulations were bogus, and they changed them accordingly. These days I hear that

Liberty students can go to movies and stay out a little later. They are treated more like adults and allowed to make their own decisions. That is how it should be. Throwing on shackles and keeping people chained to tradition for tradition's sake don't exactly nurture trust and responsibility.

Back on Track

To tell the truth, having a few more rules would have been good for me (of course, I would have had to obey them too). Eventually I got caught drinking at a party on the campus of the all-girls' school, which was bad enough, but they didn't realize I was doing pot. If that transgression had been discovered, the school's administrators never would have allowed me back; I was in enough trouble as it was. The only way out was to make a direct appeal to the dean of men to let me return the next semester.

I wanted to finish my education. I wanted to make my parents proud, to let them see that I could do it. When I came home over the break, I really had a change of heart and realized that I was heading to a place that wasn't a benefit to me or anybody else. I'd had my fill of carousing and not caring about anything. And I honestly wanted to go back and complete what I started. I created a goal for myself: finish school and then pursue my musical career. When I returned that next semester, I did everything I could to fulfill the promise I'd made to myself.

The dean of men at Liberty deserves my thanks. He was a

genuinely nice guy. I think he saw my heart and realized that I was sincere, that I wanted to come back and learn, and he allowed me that privilege. If he hadn't, my life might have turned out completely different. There is a lot to be said for compassion and forgiveness, for giving someone a second chance. I'm a big believer in second chances because I've seen God set that example.

I actually put myself on a path to meet people who would help me reach my goals and keep me out of trouble. At first it wasn't easy because those fringe people that I'd been hanging out with were interesting and fun. I can remember being wasted and laughing at some dumb joke while we were cruising down the highway in somebody's junky car. The problem was, that highway didn't lead anywhere. I always had an empty feeling at the end of the night, a feeling of wanting more than aimless fun. Because of my Christian upbringing, I knew that there was more to life, and I was determined to achieve the potential God had for me.

Not too long after I got back for the second semester of my sophomore year, I met Toby and Mike. They were looking for a singer to do some tracks on a demo tape they'd been putting together, a mix of rap and rock. It was an interesting combination, a sort of mellowed-out Beastie Boys' vibe with guitar. Although hip-hop wasn't exactly my thing, I agreed to give it a shot.

There were three songs on that first demo, and from the very beginning, something just clicked. Maybe it was the melding of rock with Run-D.M.C. rap, or maybe it was just the creative spark that seemed to arc between us whenever we got together. Whatever it was, it kept us going.

Toby and Mike were older than I was, and Toby had already graduated and was working on his master's degree. They had been friends at Liberty before I met them, and I was definitely the hired hand in the beginning. Our primary connection was the music, but after I moved into an off-campus apartment with them, we became friends.

I was working at Benetton in a mall and going to school, thinking the whole music thing was just for fun. I couldn't see it going anywhere. Maybe we'd sell a few copies of our demo to some friends on campus, but who was going to want to listen to a rap-and-rock hybrid, with Christian lyrics to boot? I was convinced that the quickest route to being noticed would

Kevin, Al Menconi, Michael Tait, Eddie DeGarmo, and Toby

be to sing about sex, drugs, and rock and roll. Toby kept sending out those tracks to Christian record companies, and before we knew it, we had an actual record contract on the table.

Because I didn't know anything about the Christian music industry, I didn't realize that nothing even remotely like what we were doing was out there. It was totally new. But I wasn't about to complain about being so pleasantly surprised at seeing that contract, and I could never have anticipated what would eventually happen through our music.

Track Four

ANGEL WITHOUT WINGS

I wanna a girl with a college head
Not some dizzy mind
I want somebody with some sentiment
You wanna waste my time

I wanna house in New Orleans
You wanna hitch a ride
So come on back when you can make some tea
And read Saint Augustine

I like the way you look outside
It's not the secrets that you try to hide
I kind of like the way you talk so tough

Chorus
There's only one road to go down
You gotta take it right out of town
She's like an angel with no wings
And don't you know she flies with strings attached

Who said romance is a chosen thing
Maybe it chose you
Who said there's someone perfect waiting in the wings
Perfection isn't you

It's not the way you look outside
It's not the boyfriend that you try to hide
I kind of like that way you stand so bold

Chorus

Oh my Lord, you can kill me where I lay
And it's alright that you sing no serenade
And it's alright, baby, that you're an angel without wings
And it's alright, girl, that you're flying with
    strings attached
Yeah

Chorus

Written by Kevin Max and Erick Cole. © 2001 Blind Thief Publishing (BMI) (admin. by
EMI CMP) / Songs from the Playground (ASCAP) (admin. by Franklin Mgmt. Group, Inc.).

ANGEL
WITHOUT WINGS

"Angel Without Wings" is about a fatal attraction to a bad girl, a woman who is disillusioned with life. The singer has fallen in love with her, knowing that she's going to be trouble because she's so insecure and needy. In the chorus the singer acknowledges that probably the best thing for him to do is to walk away from the situation, even as he admits to himself how hard that would be.

I've had a few relationships in my life in which the main attraction was an insecure feeling, a sense of danger and being on the edge. I had to come to the realization that I was just being brought down. When I was single, I seemed to have an unhealthy attraction to girls who were rebellious and pushed the envelope. It was a part of growing up and finding out what real life was about because I was raised in a very conservative home. As I ventured out on my own, I quickly recognized that most girls weren't like the ones I grew up with in church.

A line in the chorus pretty much sums up the song's point of view: "There's only one road to go down / You gotta take it right out of town." It was inspired by the many Scriptures that talk about fleeing from evil and the appearance of evil. Don't be tempted by temptation because sooner or later you're going to get in over your head and then it won't be a game anymore. It's better to close the door of your heart than to let someone who has upside-down priorities come in and mess up your life. It might be hard, but sometimes just walking away, leaving town, is the only way to protect your sanity and self-respect. "Flee from youthful lusts," Paul exhorted us in 2 Timothy 2:22, "and pursue righteousness, faith, love and peace."

"God knows we're going to get it wrong, but He has also given us the ability to get it right."

But there's another reality behind the song: it can be tough to walk away from something that's so appealing and that you want so badly. Temptation wouldn't be such an issue in our lives if the sin that tempts us didn't have a strong appeal to our all-too-human natures, if we didn't flirt with the danger of forbidden fruit and skirt the edge of God's grace. Given our natural tendency toward those enticements, we must cultivate awareness of ourselves, our strengths and weaknesses, and walk in the light, consciously staying away from situations that may be more than we can handle and that we may not be able to get ourselves out of.

Control Freak

The trouble starts when we think we're in control of ourselves, our emotions, and our choices. I've said it before, but it's worth repeating: life is about learning from mistakes, and I've made my share, so I know what I'm talking about. The point is that we learn and avoid having to repeat the same lessons again and again. God knows we're going to get it wrong, but He has also given us the ability to get it right. And He has given us the responsibility to take those life lessons to heart so that we can make progress toward being better and, I hope, wiser people.

If we constantly give in to temptation, our lives become very predictable, even though for the moment they can seem exciting and unconventional. But if we sacrifice those alluring things we think we want in those moments, the material things and the emotional things, we can lay a foundation for peace and security in our lives that will allow us to accomplish the real goals and challenges that have been set before us.

Some people don't like to hear it, but there really is wisdom in moderation, in self-control, and in not running too far in one direction or the other. For me, the issue of alcohol is a perfect analogy. I enjoy having a glass or two of a fine wine. It's one of the small pleasures of life. But if you drink two bottles, afterward I guarantee you'll feel like an idiot. "Wine is a mocker," Proverbs 20:1 declares, "strong drink a brawler, and whoever is intoxicated by it is not wise."

It's really between you and God to establish the limits for

yourself. And that requires an honest ability to listen and respond to the voice of your conscience. Too many of us let someone else dictate hard-and-fast rules that we're supposed to live by, and to me, that's nothing more than spiritual intimidation.

Once I was at a club having a good time, not overdoing it or making a spectacle of myself; I was just enjoying the company of my fiancée and unwinding a little. A photographer happened to be there, and he took a picture of me with a cigar in one hand and a beer in the other, with my arm around Alayna. It ended up in a magazine, and people immediately assumed that I was a wild party animal. Before I knew it, the picture was all over the Internet, and people were up in arms, asking if I was the sort of individual that parents wanted to set an example for their kids. I was held up as a bad role model.

Maybe that's all true. Maybe drinking in public is the worst thing someone in my position can do. Maybe that one picture was a stumbling block for thousands of kids who used it to justify their own bad behavior. And maybe being in the media spotlight brings with it the responsibility that requires me to be sensitive to everyone else's concerns and moral codes. I can't argue with that, except to say that those accusations were very tough for me to deal with because my conscience tells me that drinking in moderation isn't wrong. I truly enjoy going out and talking to friends over a drink. Relaxation and stimulating conversation are hard enough to come by in this stressed-out world.

It hurt me that people wanted to take that freedom away

Alayna and Kevin Max, Nashville style

from me. And it was even more painful to try to communicate my point of view to them because they were so dead set against hearing anything other than their own opinion reflected to them. Their minds were made up.

Some people in the Christian music industry wanted to take every dc Talk record off the shelves. And in the end I went before a board of those people and told them that I was sorry, I'd be careful in the future, and I'd submit to the need to be more circumspect in public about what I do and how it's perceived.

Invasion of Privacy

But in retrospect I've got to admit that I still don't think what I did was wrong for me. I acted according to the dictates of my conscience, and I'm as answerable to God for my behavior as any bunch of people who sit in judgment of me. I wonder if they ever thought about taking the Bible off the shelf because it's a book that describes people drinking wine, with Jesus right there in their midst. Or maybe they'd like to publish a nonalcoholic version of the wedding party at Cana. Maybe they aren't aware that C. S. Lewis, one of the great Christian apologists of our time, was known to hoist a few down at the local pub with his cronies. It was part of the academic culture around Oxford University, where he taught at that time, and it still is. I would have been honored to have been able to have a beer with those learned men and listen to their talk about literature and poetry and maybe the local cricket match.

To me, it's obvious that drinking isn't a spiritual issue. What rules your life is a spiritual issue. And as much as people can become addicted to alcohol, they can become addicted to the power of telling the rest of us how to live our lives. I've never tried to purposely offend anybody. And while it's true that when I step out of my door in the morning I need to be more aware than most people about the possible effects of my behavior, I might as well stay locked up in the house if that's what's going to rule my life. At some point, sooner or later, no matter how hard I try to avoid it, I'm probably going to do something that somebody isn't going to like. And if, as a result, that person is going to launch a crusade to discourage kids from listening to my music, then I guess I'll have to live with the consequences.

> "Drinking isn't a spiritual issue. what rules your life is a spiritual issue."

I can't stop people from taking pictures of me. I can't stop the invasion of privacy that seems to be more and more a part of our society. I want to be careful about the message I'm sending to young kids. I don't want to be a spokesperson for the liquor industry, but even more important that that, I want kids to develop the ability to judge right and wrong for themselves on the issue of drinking or anything else that might confront them in the real world. To parents and youth pastors I would say, treat kids as if you trust them, and honor their individuality. Listen to what they're saying, answer their questions honestly, and don't judge them for having to make tough choices in this world.

Family Values

Parents need to do their duty, first and foremost, and when they do, I think a lot of these issues will be placed in their proper perspective. I'm not saying it's easy to raise kids in the environment we face today, but that's no excuse not to try. I have no problem with parents teaching their kid that drinking is wrong if that's what they truly believe. And I have no problem with them enforcing that belief as long as they have responsibility for their child.

But isn't the whole point of parenting to bring a child to the place where he can make up his own mind? Don't we want children to think for themselves, decide for themselves, and act from their own free will? Too many of us want the government, the church, or some role model that's been set up as the ultimate example of righteous behavior to tell us what to do. That's just refusing to take responsibility on a one-to-one basis with kids. And that's where the real trouble begins.

It's an issue I've seen from both sides. My birth father was a product of the sixties, when nobody felt he had the right to tell anyone else how to live his life. The result was a broken home and real emotional jeopardy. On the other hand, my adoptive dad was very outspoken about what he thought I should or should not do. I learned to respect that, which doesn't mean that I always agreed with it, but I submitted when I was under his roof because he was paying the bills and providing for me and creating an environment in which I could grow to maturity and feel secure. When I left that environment, my choices became my responsibility, and I came up with my own solutions to problems I faced, solutions that were more often than not grounded in the values he taught me.

Generally speaking, the family used to be much stronger than it is today. Parents need to be more educated about what their kids are into and what they're up to, and then it wouldn't come as such a surprise when they discover that their sons or daughters are facing choices that they might not have had to deal with as young people.

Sure, some kids can be very deceptive and totally pull the wool over the parents' eyes. I know. I was one of them. I'd tell my mom and dad that I was going over to a friend's house when I was really heading for a field party, trying to meet girls. I was doing things that they didn't know about and never found out about—at least I don't think they did. Maybe they knew all the time and just decided that I needed to learn my own lessons in my own way. And that's the real point. My parents provided the framework by which I could evaluate what is right and wrong. That is exactly why I eventually came to the realization that living a double life was betraying not only them but also my own values.

Today, too many parents seem frightened to set up guidelines for their kids. But it's more important now than ever. Proverbs 13:1 lays it right out for us: "A wise son accepts his father's discipline, but a scoffer does not listen to rebuke." It's a dangerous world out there, and whether we like it or not, the environment of kidnapping and molestation and violence really puts limits on our freedom. If I had a kid, I'm sure I'd be a little nervous every time he walked out the door. It's not the kid's fault. It's the fault of a world that has turned away from God, which is exactly why some parents find it easier to let their kids run their own lives. They're worried about not being friends with their sons or daughters; they're worried that the kids won't like them if they're too strict. So they abdicate their authority and squander the respect that every child naturally feels for his parents.

> "God created families as crucibles to forge our characters . . . In a family our own love and commitment are tested on a daily basis."

Let's face it. Raising kids, without shuffling off the job to some government official or authority figure, is a real balancing act. The structure has to be there—the rules of right and wrong, and the respect necessary to enforce those rules. But at the same time, every mother and father has to practice grace, to be able to stand aside and allow kids to experience life for themselves, even if that experience is painful.

God created families as crucibles to forge our characters. The relationships of a parent to a child, a brother to a sister, and a husband to a wife are among the most challenging and rewarding that we'll ever know. Friends come and go. God's relationship to us is eternal. But in a family our own love and commitment are tested on a daily basis. We create our own heavens and hells. We coexist in the darkness of denial or the light of honest self-examination. In the family our values are established, our characters are formed, and our sense of self is built up or torn down.

I can't speak from experience about raising children, but I do know about being married. It's the most rewarding, and most demanding, connection a person can ever make with another human being.

There are also aspects of being married that can be humbling. And I speak from firsthand experience. I'd be out on the road, being lavished with praise from people telling me what they thought I wanted to hear. Then sometimes I'd come home, and Alayna would be mad at me because I forgot to call her that day. Or she'd be upset because she could see that I hadn't been taking care of myself as well as I should. When that happened, it was a real reality check, and I'd come down off my superstar high right away. Over the years, I've learned to appreciate the grounding that she provides me. If I lived my life

Househusband

basking in praises 24/7, how would I ever realize my weaknesses and work on minimizing them?

In the Spotlight

Being in dc Talk was another major source of humility and one that taught me some valuable lessons. I'd always thought of myself as the lead character in any musical enterprise, the one who called the shots. Then suddenly I was part of a team with two other guys who were equally intent on being in charge. It was a real adjustment, and a lot of ego deflating was involved. For instance, Toby and Mike used to dance up front onstage, and since I just wasn't any good at synchronized dancing, I'd step back and play keyboard behind them as they did their thing. That took some getting used to because I naturally wanted to be out in the spotlight, too, up front singing to the people. For a long time, I had to be content with being a supporting player. But that also grounded me and made me a better performer.

dc Talk is a very competitive group, and I think that makes us an interesting band, especially live. Onstage it's all about interacting with the crowd, and no one totally takes over the stage. We're all front and center—or trying to be. And as you can imagine, that competitiveness can make for some problems on occasion. But on the whole, I think Toby and Mike and I get along remarkably well. We are like brothers in a sense, and how many brothers do you know who don't argue and disagree once in a while?

When we finally got off the road after the *Supernatural* tour, I decided I wanted to do some solo acoustic dates just to get back in touch with my own music, appearing in coffee-houses and churches and places where I'd have a chance to talk to people one-on-one. And I have to admit that, after appearing in front of sold-out crowds of ten thousand or more, playing for a handful of customers in a dark cabaret was a very hum-bling experience. Yet it made me work that much harder to connect with those fifty people staring right at me than I had to with the five thousand who were shouting and waving their hands in the air off in the darkness of an arena.

"dc Talk is a very competitive group, and I think that makes us an interesting band."

I guess what I'm trying to say is that wisdom comes in many guises, and it's a wise man who can see the value in simple humbleness. It's an eternal quality, and it brings us face-to-face with our need for God. We know we're going to die. We know we're getting older and slowing down. And if we're honest with ourselves, we know we're imperfect. At any second we could sin, telling a lie instead of telling the truth, being cruel instead of being kind. Knowing that we have the capacity to be jerks is humbling. And in that humility we learn how to put others first and be of service to our fellowman. To excel, we have to sacrifice, do things that we don't want to do—things that sometimes may be painful, things that may take more work than we're willing to put into them. That's what excellence is all about. There's not a single person I know who has become successful without making sacrifices.

But even if we work and sacrifice and struggle for our dreams, there's no guarantee that they're going to come true. Let's be straight about it. Not all of us, when we finally make that true connection with ourselves, are going be transformed into superstars. And this world conveys the message that if you're not a superstar, you're nobody. That's a lie. The whole of humanity is made up of many separate parts and different individuals. Not everybody can be Martin Luther King or Bono or Tiger Woods. Not everybody can be president of the United States.

Paul painted a vivid picture in Romans 12:4–5 when he said, "Just as we have many members in one body and all the members do not have the same function, so we, who are many, are one body in Christ." Different people excel in different ways to different degrees. It may seem obvious, but we need to be constantly reminded that we have value, just as we are.

Lofty Goals

In some people's minds, I'm a superstar. They might wonder whether I could be satisfied playing my songs in front of fifty people a night instead of five thousand. My answer to that is simple. I have lofty goals. But there are other people, maybe including you, who can attain their goals in front of fifty people or in front of no people. We need to ask ourselves how we can best fulfill God's plan for our lives and not always be looking at someone else's example or experience. Van Gogh probably knew he was a great artist, or he wouldn't have continued with his work. Yet he never sold a painting in his life. What kept him going was the joy of doing what he was born to do.

That self-expression can be intensely personal. I have to admit that everyone wants to be acknowledged and recognized. That's a natural human need. So the question you've got to ask yourself is, *How can I best be recognized and appreciated?* By doing what you think is going to attract people's attention, or by practicing and polishing the gifts and talents God has given you in the first place?

> "If we can realize our *true value,* our purpose within God's plan becomes a lot more clear and concise."

My goals may be ambitious, but I truly believe God has equipped me to accomplish them. I want to be able to entertain people and, by entertaining them, to provoke them to thought. I want to challenge them into becoming better at being themselves. I want to inspire them, and I think God has given me a platform and a passion to do that work. To me, that means He has a purpose for me in mind.

What I'm trying to say about myself is true for all of us. If we can realize our true value, our purpose within God's plan becomes a lot more clear and concise. Then God can use us more effectively. That isn't the same as saying that God needs us to get His job done. I meet many people who get caught up in the fantasy that God needs them to accomplish His work of salvation. Hey, God can do that all by Himself. But He does use people who are usable, and that privilege comes with being willing to submit to His direction and guidance.

I like to consider myself more usable than I probably am sometimes. There are days when I wake up totally ready for what He has in store. Other days He's probably thinking, *Well, Kevin's doing his thing right now. I'll come back later.* We're like children in that way. You teach your kid the right thing and he gets it; he does what he's supposed to do. But then he forgets it the next time and screws up. As a parent, you love him regardless and teach him the right way all over again. You want to show him what he can do. You want to show him what he can be. But it takes time and discipline and sometimes correction and humbling.

What's true for me is true for you. But the good news is that, beyond the humbling experiences that God allows us to go through, a powerful new sense of purpose and power comes from knowing who you are in relation to God and in relation to the world in which He's placed you. I've talked about my "lofty goals," but all of us can reach the stars if we look to God to lift us up when we're ready.

Track Five

SHAPING SPACE

And they said we wouldn't last
And they said the years would break our backs
So here we are again, my friend
To mystify their narrow plans

You and I were meant to be
Much more than they could see
You and I were meant to stay
As they waste away

Chorus
We are shaping the spaces
And harvesting places
We're the princes of the universe
We are living together
In the here-everafter
In the temple of the evening Son
We're the princes of the universe

It's a prophecy of long ago
It's a blueprint for the journey home
And we're writing as we stumble on
Making history to build upon

You and I were meant to be
Much more than they could see
You and I are meant to stay
As we'll waste away

Chorus

And the raven in the tower clock
Spins poetry and devil talk, and the woman by the
    endless well
She's drawing water from the mouth of hell
"And these are the days," she says and

Chorus

Written by Kevin Max. © 2001 Blind Thief Publishing (BMI) (admin. by EMI CMP).

"Shaping Space" came to me as I was singing in the shower one day. As soon as I had the idea, I immediately started working on the lyrics. It was pure stream of consciousness, more like a poem than the verses and a chorus to a song, and it was only later that I went back to my keyboard and shaped the music to the words.

I produced this album with the help of Adrian Belew and a few close collaborators. Although some recording artists will tell you that they need the feedback from another set of ears, producing my own music is pretty easy for me because I know exactly what I want, exactly what I'm going for, and exactly how to execute it. I had definite ideas from the very beginning of where I wanted to go with each song, but a big part of the whole process in the studio is to leave room for surprises and new inspiration. Sometimes the material will take a direction I didn't expect, and I can't be so boxed into my ideas that I can't break out and allow for new approaches. Most of the time when surprises happen, the result is better than what I originally had in mind.

"Shaping Space" is a good example. I initially recorded the track with a piano, and as it came out, it sounded a lot like "Imagine" by John Lennon. It was a little too close for comfort, so I added different drums and a horn section, and it took on a completely different feel.

I've always been a huge John Lennon fan. The sound of his voice, his wit, and the musical hooks he came up with had an enormous influence on me. And in some of his later solo work, I could really hear the voice of someone who was asking honest questions about important issues. "Imagine" itself came from

Getting the studio blues with Adrian Belew and Erick Cole

Central Park, Strawberry Fields 2001

an interesting point of view spiritually, particularly when he asked us to "imagine there's no heaven." I think he was painting a very idealistic picture of some form of communism where we could live together on the same economic plane, loving and working as one, all wearing the same clothes, nobody better than anyone else. It's a little weird, but I understand where he was coming from.

Lennon had a hard time living without absolutes, and in that regard I was always surprised that he wasn't able to go farther in a spiritual direction. But what he *was* able to do instead was to grab spirituality from everyday places and things. He didn't learn it or practice it, but he was able to discover deeper meaning in things such as his love for Yoko and the belief that he had found in her his soul mate. As a married man who's very much in love with his wife, I relate to that completely.

Apocalyptic Imagery

In its own way "Shaping Space" is my attempt to grab at spiritual truth. The song is a statement about heaven, about eternity, and about how I believe that we all can get there. When I say in the song that we're "the princes of the universe," I mean that to realize our destiny is to realize our greatness. We can overcome the limitations of this world because we have access to a higher power. We can look forward to something beyond death, to being in a better place and existing in a perfected state. Scripture says that there will be no hunger, no war, and no fear. We will be in a glorified state.

I think when they hear that description of eternity, some people imagine something boring. But I think it's going to be just the opposite. How exciting it will be to fully and totally *be* who we were meant to be, living in the complete awareness of our intimate relationship with the Creator of the universe!

In the song I try to give a picture of what I think the end times will be like. When I sing about "the raven in the tower clock" and "the woman by the endless well," I'm drawing on the apocalyptic imagery of the book of Revelation,

> "To realize our **destiny** is to realize our **greatness.** We can **overcome** the limitations of this world because we have access to a **higher power."**

which talks a lot about what will happen in the future. People will have to endure a time of tribulation before the Great Judgment when all our thoughts and deeds will be weighed and measured against God's standards. It's open to interpretation, of course, but some aspects are clear and unequivocal. Christ will come again and set up His kingdom here on earth. God will change the very nature of our existence and redeem our physical bodies, just as He redeems the earth.

Many people are out there searching, but not finding what they're looking for. It's almost as if they are staring at their own reflection in a pool of water and can't see past it to the depths beneath. The ultimate truth of reality, as far as I can discern, lies in our relationship with God, and that relationship is mirrored every day, in the here and now, in our faith and our trust in the goodness and mercy of the Lord.

Just as I did with so many of the songs on this album, I wrote "Shaping Space" with Alayna in mind. When we first got married, there were those, such as her parents, who were doubtful, knowing that the lifestyle of a musician is hard on any relationship. Think about what happened with my birth parents. But Alayna and I have something they never did—a strong spiritual connection. What keeps us together and keeps our marriage healthy is our shared belief in God and His purpose for our lives.

If we didn't have that, it would be tough, and I honestly don't believe we would make it. Faith has set us apart. It has made us more committed to each other and to growing together than anything we could have achieved on our own. I hope that doesn't sound self-righteous, as if we think we're better than everybody else. What God has given us, He wants to give to all His creatures. We are His sons and daughters. We have that inheritance.

Transforming Destiny

But it's up to us to lay hold of that inheritance. The title of the song and the refrain "shaping the spaces and harvesting places" are all about working here on earth, within the confines of this life, toward the ultimate goal of heaven. The things that I do on earth will come to fruition in eternity. But I also wanted to leave the song open-ended so that the meaning wouldn't be immediately accessible. I wanted people to draw their own conclusions and make the application to their lives. Some might conclude that it's about how we act and what we say in everyday life that matters. That's how we shape the space around us. And they'd be right.

What I do with my relationships and in the community of which I'm a member helps to shape that space, just as my personal decisions alter and transform the shape of my destiny. The central message of the song is that it is important in life to have a positive influence. The more negative consequences you trigger, the fewer places you can go in your own space and the fewer places you allow other people to go. "Bless those who curse you," Jesus said in Luke 6:28, "pray for those who mistreat you."

You don't even have to look at it as some kind of spiritual analogy. Christians may immediately read that meaning into it, which is okay, too, but I really meant it in a very broad sense. It may be about getting to heaven, but it's also about bringing a little bit of heaven down here to earth. I want to make my wife happy and give her what she wants, which is one way of shaping the space around the two of us. But I'm also shaping our space when I come home and I'm selfish and egotistical and isolated. When I'm like that, I'm making things smaller and darker and more cramped.

For example, I'm not really excited about having social evenings, but Alayna loves having people over to the house. It's one of the things we disagreed over when we first got married until I decided that, because I love her, I wanted to give her the things she desires. I was able to shape a space that was

At dinner with friends Peter and Summer Furler

comfortable for her, and as a result, she responded by being more sensitive to my need for solitude. Together we created an environment where we could comfortably coexist.

The words to "Shaping Space" came to me very quickly, which is true for several songs on my album. Songwriting is a very spontaneous process, and once I get going I can usually complete an entire song in half an hour. If I have a melody, I can usually craft the lyrics and sing the tune in my head even as I write them out on paper. It's a very rapid process, and if I need to change something when it is time to record, I'll take a few words out or put a few in, but that's rare. Most often, the words come out as a whole.

The music is often more challenging. I can get stuck on something for months at a time, trying to perfect the melody or arrangement. My primary gift is coming up with the words, which is why I consider myself first and foremost a poet. When I get into the flow of that gift, it's one of the most satisfying feelings I've ever had. It puts a smile on my face. It's like the smile everyone gets when he knows he's doing what he's meant to do.

Fed by Ravens

Because I have a love of words and poetry, more than anything I'd like to be known as a poet, even more than a songwriter. Poetry comes from the soul and speaks to the soul, and it really doesn't matter if I get rich or famous from writing poems. I do it for the sake of doing it, for giving my truest and deepest voice a means of expression, and that's all the justification I'll ever need.

I have always found more freedom in poetry than in song lyrics, which have a very definite structure. As a musician, I know it's important to consider how I can reach the greatest number of people in a way that as many as possible will understand. Don't get me wrong. I appreciate the

> "When we're expressing what's true for us, no matter how we do it, it's a supernatural act because we're exercising a talent that comes directly from God."

fact that I have the ability to craft accessible music. After all, I have to make a living. But I also appreciate what the gifted poet e. e. cummings said about the art form: "Poets should be fed by the ravens."

When we're expressing what's true for us, no matter how we do it, it's a supernatural act because we're exercising a talent that comes directly from God. Each of us needs to take the time to discover our gifts; we need to figure them out and then get better at them.

The love of words and music was one of my first conscious realizations. I couldn't walk into a bookstore without wanting to leave with ten different volumes about everything under the sun. I couldn't put a pen in my hand without wanting to write something down. I couldn't listen to a song without wanting to sing along. Maybe God has gifted me in that area more than He has other people, but my belief is that He created us all on a very level playing field. Each of us may have different skills and abilities, but the reason we've been given these abilities is exactly the same in each case. It's God's way of infusing us with a passion for living, a way to find peace and joy and fulfillment in our lives.

These goals are attainable for each of us, but it's also true that God gives certain people special gifts at specific times for particular reasons. It's not that He loves some people more than others; it's just that He has a definite use in mind when He endows them with their unique combination of skills and artistry.

Think of King David. You've got to wonder why God

showed a lowly shepherd so much favor, even after David messed up so badly. You've got to wonder why He showed David so much love, even after he was king and committed adultery and murder. But David was described as a man after God's own heart, and God recognized and honored that quality, even in the midst of serious sin.

I would venture to say that David realized his gifts very early in his life and knew what he was about right from the start. How else could he have gained the wisdom and inspiration to write so many immortal poems of such profound understanding? He knew what he was made for, what he was called to do, and how to accomplish his goals.

It might not have been easy. It never is. If you think you have a message for your generation, it's never too early to start trying to get it out there because you'd better believe there are going to be obstacles and roadblocks and setbacks that will discourage you and try to deflect you from that mission. But it's the difficulty that makes the job worth doing. If it was easy, anyone could go for it.

So You Wanna Be a Rock and Roll Star?

If I had a son or daughter who wanted to go into the music business, I would completely support the decision. And if my child showed any aptitude, I'd want to make sure there was a miniature drum kit or a toy piano in the house for him or her to start banging around on. Music is such a big a part of who I am, and it has brought me so much freedom and happiness, that if one of my own flesh and blood wanted to follow in my footsteps, I don't think anything would make me happier.

Nevertheless, I'd want my child to be completely aware of what he was getting into as part of the recording industry. *Disillusionment* is a strong word, but there have been plenty of times when I've been angry and saddened by the treatment artists are given by the businessmen who control the levers of power. What bothers me the most is what bothers me in every other aspect of life: dishonesty in people.

> *"I'm not frightened of rejection because I believe in what I do and I also believe that someone, sooner or later, will catch the vision."*

Someone who has given all his time and energy to making music is owed an honest response from the people who can put it out there for a mass audience. Giving a straight-up evaluation is much better than leading an artist on and making him think that something will happen when it isn't even going to be given a chance. Anyone who wants to be part of this world has to understand that the music business is, first and foremost, a business. It's about the money and trying to make as much as possible from an artist and his life's work. If you get that firmly in your head, it will be a lot harder to get your feelings hurt. (A friend of mine in the business once said, "music business—small *m*, big *B*.")

I'm not frightened of rejection because I believe in what I

do and I also believe that someone, sooner or later, will catch the vision. I've also surrounded myself with trustworthy, first-rate people, people who can help make my music an appealing commodity in the business world.

But I don't have time for people tickling my ear, telling me what they think I want to hear. Most of them are just covering their bets, not wanting to lose the opportunity to stay connected with me in case I should hit it big. They're wasting their time and mine.

Dozens of e-mails and letters arrive every week from people asking me how to make it in the music industry. I try to be as honest as possible with my advice. It's simple really: develop yourself as a songwriter and as an entertainer. Try to get some experience in a studio, and play for as many people as you can. Beyond that, it's out of your hands, and if you're not meant to survive in the music world, you'll find out soon enough.

Along with practicing your craft and improving your art, I say that it's about drive and ambition. If you don't have the will to succeed against all odds, then you're going to get chewed up because there are so many other people who want the same thing and may want it even more. dc Talk has been very fortunate to establish a reputation over the years and build a loyal following, but the greatest blessing of all is that we've been able to do it with a minimum of compromise in our business dealings and in the music we make. We've continued to evolve as a group, and we've never worried about losing our fan base. We can change stylistically from record to record, and people have followed along with us and have brought along their friends too.

We've managed to stay interesting and challenging, and I'm convinced that the reason is that we're three very different guys with three very different forms of expression. Magic happens when we come together, an unexplained phenomenon that occurs whenever we're onstage together. I'm not drawing comparisons necessarily, but I think it's the combination of different personalities and talents that accounts for the appeal of a band such as the Beatles, where every fan had a favorite member, yet the sum of the whole was greater than the parts. Oasis is another good example of what I'm talking about. I don't think that group would be half as interesting if it weren't for those two brothers fighting and feuding all the time. The members, as much as the music, make a band great.

Great bands and great music aren't easy to come by, especially in Christian music these days. Originality counts for me, but I hear too many Christian versions of mainstream artists who, in turn, are pale imitations of someone else. I like to listen to a group like U2. Whether they are card-carrying Christians, I couldn't say, but there is definitely a spiritual perspective to what they're doing. There's just no other way of putting it. They're singing about grace and mercy and truth, and these subjects, to me, embody the Christian ethic. But most important, the guys are totally sincere about what they're saying, which boils down to one simple message: there can be something more to your life.

The way I look at it, it's no use trying to limit how God uses somebody's talents to make an impact in popular culture, whether you want to call the person a "Christian." There will always be artists who come along to push and prod people and get them to think about spiritual realities. It's like a cycle that repeats itself. Dylan started one of those cycles, bringing up Christian concepts in his music, and because he was a poet and a thinker, that eventually led him to a personal experience with God. I really believe the times are right for somebody else to come along and start the cycle again. It could be me. It could even be you.

Kmax and Tony Levin

Track Six

DEAD END MOON

As the sand shifts cool beneath your feet
By the light of a dead end moon
Your haunted fingers on my skin so sweet
Your hair the darkest loom

Like a cherub left to gather moss
Like a ship without its sail that's tossed
Like a vassal to his kingdom lost
My soul so pale
Oh my lonely heart
Oh my soulless girl, will you ever let me go?

I don't wanna cry no more
And here I wander aimless
I just want to find the cure
To my growing weakness
And the one who wanders is not lost, my friend

From on top a Moorish wall I stand
I see the valley stretching
The mist of seas are pulling in
From your cliff I'm stranded
Embedded in your body deep

Lie answers to the questions
Like a garden hidden from the keep
How long I've waited

Oh my lonely heart
Oh my soulless girl, will you ever let me go?

I don't wanna cry no more
And here I wander aimless
I just want to find the cure
To my growing weakness

Oh dark mistress, my only salvation
If only to hold you in blessed suspension
Eyes that hold midnight, smile that brings out light
Strange fascination, my only placation

I don't wanna cry no more
And here I wander aimlessly
I just want to find the cure
To this infernal sadness

Written by Kevin Max and Mark "Cinco" Townshend. © 2001 Blind Thief Publishing (BMI) (admin. by EMI CMP) / Vesper Records (ASCAP).

"Dead End Moon" is a cut where the music matters almost as much to me as the lyrics, at least when it comes to expressing the meaning and intent of the song.

As with many of the selections on my album, I worked on the music with my good friend and collaborator Mark "Cinco" Townshend, who not only provides me with great musical ideas that serve as a launch point for the music, but also is great at taking even the vaguest suggestion for a theme or direction and turning it into a living, breathing reality. While songwriting for me is ultimately a very personal expression and a solitary endeavor, the act of creating the actual song, improvising onstage, or crafting it in the studio requires the talents and cooperation of any number of people. It's important to have a team that I can trust and depend on, and Cinco and Erick Cole are at the forefront of my particular posse. This album wouldn't have existed without their inspiration and energy.

On its most basic level, "Dead End Moon" is a song about romance and denial, about wanting something that is just out of reach, not being able to grab on to it, but at the same time, not being willing to stop trying. We've all been there, whether it's a person we've created some elaborate fantasy about, or some goal or ambition that we think will bring us complete fulfillment. We believe that, because we want it so badly, we're somehow entitled to have it, as if desire were all it took to create reality. We won't listen when friends try to tell us that we're fooling ourselves. We deny the evidence that's right in front of us. We hope against hope that somehow it's going to work out the way we want.

Beautiful Delusions

And when it doesn't, we watch helplessly as our world comes tumbling down. The prospect of dealing with disappointment is more than some of us can handle, but experiencing failure and savoring success are necessary for spiritual growth. I've spoken often in this book about being who we are meant to be, reaching for something that may seem as if it's out of reach and risking being let down in order to achieve more than we can imagine. But the truth is, we're not always going to get what we want, just as we're not all going to become rich and famous and influential. What we make of that inevitability is what's important. God will give us disappointments as surely as He will bless us, and sometimes they come wrapped in the same package.

What matters is our response. Allowing ourselves to be crushed by failures in our lives is no more productive than pretending that failures will never happen. Worse still is an attitude that I've seen way too often, the one that won't allow us to try to go for something because of the possibility that we might not achieve the goal. We become bitter and cynical about our prospects for success, and our anticipation of blessing from a loving God turns instead to an expectation of a negative response from a vengeful and vindictive God. We resent

> "Experiencing *failure* and *savoring success* are necessary for *spiritual growth.*"

other people's successes and are envious of their talents and abilities and what they have been able to make out of them. In 1 Peter 2:1 we're told in no uncertain terms to put "aside all malice and all deceit and hypocrisy and envy and all slander."

Being in a successful group, I've had to face all those things from people who didn't want anyone else to have something that they didn't. They had given up trying, and they wanted to deny others the opportunity for success. I just don't have any patience with that attitude. Envy is more than a destructive emotion; it can become an all-consuming obsession that will eat away at the time and energy needed to actually do something worthwhile.

And what's true about personal ambition is also true about relationships. "Dead End Moon" is a poetic picture of the kind of longing that one person can have for another that takes him to that empty, lonely place where life becomes a barren pursuit of some unattainable ideal. So much of the art and entertainment of our culture, and many other cultures throughout history, is about falling in love, as if love were a deep pit that we stumble into, never to emerge again. We've been led to believe that if we could only possess the perfect image of a dream lover, we would transcend this mundane existence and live in an eternal ecstasy of romantic bliss.

That delusion is a guarantee of disappointment. Even if we find the supposed individual who represents the "perfect" ideal, the chances are, we're not going to fill the same role for that person. And on the slim chance that we do, the concept that any individual can bring complete happiness and ultimate meaning to our lives is an example of the fractured thinking that's behind every celebrity stalker out there, chasing a celluloid fantasy. It's a frightening commentary on our world when people begin to believe in image more than the person behind the image. In my career I'm always struggling to connect with others as a flesh-and-blood human being and not just a projection of some rock and roll wish fulfillment.

Mystifying Music

The underlying issue once more comes down to knowing who we really are as individuals created in God's image for His unique purpose. When we become shadows of ourselves, unattached from our intrinsic value, we are seduced into accepting substitutes for real life with all its promises and problems, triumphs and travails. Being firmly rooted in our unique identity, as it has been established by God, is the only way we're going to be able to objectively deal with disappointments, to be able to turn away from what is beyond us and look toward what we can accomplish.

I'm a firm believer that our reach should always exceed, at least a little, our grasp. There should always be something we're striving to achieve. And if we're meant to lay hold of whatever it is, whether it's a person, a possession, or a passionate ideal, God will give us the means to reach it. It's always worth remembering that what He has laid aside for us is greater and more amazing than anything we could imagine for ourselves.

> *"I'm a firm believer that our reach should always exceed, at least a little, our grasp."*

But as I said earlier, the real significance of "Dead End Moon" is not so much in the meaning of the words but in the feelings evoked by the music. The song creates a pivotal moment in the sequence of this record, embodying a kind of mystery and intrigue that I wanted to infuse into all the music. It's not something I can put into precise words. Yet everything from the chord changes to the time signature, the melody to the arrangement, articulates an aura that is very much at the core of my creative vision.

You don't have to listen very hard to pick up a distinct Eastern flavor in the music of "Dead End Moon." That probably had something to do with the fact that I was very heavily into George Harrison's landmark solo album, *All Things Must Pass*, at the time. And that, in turn, most likely goes back to the fascination with the East that I may have picked up from my birth father.

Whatever the case, the art and culture of the East have continued to exert an influence on me through most of my musical career. While incorporating those influences into my songwriting comes naturally without any conscious intent, I would have to say that the obvious Eastern aspects of "Dead End Moon" were motivated, at least in part, by my desire to move listeners out of their familiar stylistic comfort zones.

And it's not just matters of musical taste that cause some people to become uncomfortable when talk turns to the East. Try to bring up the ancient and enduring wisdom of that part of planet Earth, and watch the reaction. It's simultaneously amazing and alarming to me that Western Christians are so ready to dismiss, right out of hand, the faith and belief systems of half the world.

All Truth Is God's Truth

I can hear the objections now: "Jesus Christ said that He was the way, the truth, and the life, and no man could come to the Father except through Him." Let me be clear: I believe that 100 percent. I'm *not* saying there is more than one way to God. But I am saying I believe there is value in understanding and even respecting the faith of others instead of remaining ignorant about it or ridiculing it.

Understand, I think it's the responsibility of every believer to pray that the full light of God's truth will be revealed to all mankind. In the meantime, I think we should try to understand the historical, cultural, and social conditions in which much of the rest of the world exists. It's hard for me to accept the arrogant, dismissive attitude of some Christians toward followers of other religions.

> "I believe that Christ was the Son of God, sent from heaven to save man by the ultimate act of sacrifice on the cross."

I don't know that I can answer the questions my opinions might raise, but I'm sure that asking them doesn't make me any less a Christian. I know that some people would answer by saying that it is our responsibility, through the call of the Great Commission, to preach the gospel to those who live in darkness, and I'm all for spreading the light of Jesus to the farthest corners of the earth. But it seems to me that before we can preach salvation to people, we've got to at least try to understand them as individuals with a history and heritage all their own, deserving, at the very least, our respect.

Too many Christians behave as if even approaching a thoughtful and honest exchange with someone of another religion is akin to inviting the devil over for dinner. Of course, we have to learn what we're up against if we intend to lead an Eastern man to the foot of the cross. But I would suggest that it's vital for us to be educated for another reason. "The truth will make you free," states John 8:32. If we can identify some piece of God's truth in what followers of other faiths believe, we will have discovered common ground that just might lead them to spiritual freedom.

I'm not saying that all paths lead to God, or that Jesus was just another holy man like Buddha or Confucius. I believe that Christ was the Son of God, sent from heaven to save man by the ultimate act of sacrifice on the cross. I've had too many encounters with that reality to doubt it. Yet I want to listen with respect and learn what followers of other religions believe as firmly and as adamantly as I believe in Jesus.

Like Eastern music, Eastern thought and philosophy are complex and sophisticated and full of nuance and hidden meaning. I want to learn everything I can about them so that I can intelligently share what I know. I think you should consider the same approach. Don't ignore or make fun of people whose beliefs differ from yours. Listen to them with respect and compassion. In time, you just may build a bridge of faith that will change their lives.

Track Seven

UNION OF SOULS

How can I be so despairing
when you are so full of joy?
How can I be so laser-like
and you so passively content?
Why must I bleed my sorrows
while you hide your accomplishments?
Why must I wallow in the mire

when you fly above it all?
I struggle with a word of truth
but you would wither if a lie passed your teeth
How can I be me, and you be you?
It is the union
that makes us whole
separately in control of each other.

Written by Kevin Max. © 2001 Blind Thief Publishing (BMI) (admin. by EMI CMP).

"Union of Souls" is a change of pace from the rest of the CD. It's an interlude, a chance for you as the listener to catch your breath a little and get ready for what you might call the second act of the album. It's the shortest track I recorded, a little more than a minute, and it's also more of a poem set to music than a synthesis of melody and lyrics. I've had poems on dc Talk albums before, such as the hidden track on *Jesus Freak*, so I'm sort of carrying on a tradition here.

On the simplest level "Union of Souls" is about the love between my wife and me. I've tried to write truthfully about how my weakness is overcome through her strength and vice versa.

If I were to evaluate the two of us, I'd have to say that I stumble more in my personal life than Alayna does in hers. For instance, I'm prone to exaggeration, which is something she would never do. On the other hand, as I said earlier, she's sometimes not overtly sensitive to my need for solitude. Like the partners in any marriage, neither of us is perfect. But I do believe that there is a unique aspect to my relationship with Alayna. Maybe because I was thrust into the spotlight so early with dc Talk, it's sometimes difficult for me to see my faults and flaws clearly. She has helped me to honestly evaluate myself, learn how to get rid of old baggage, and adopt a more positive attitude.

> "His purpose for our lives is a reflection of His presence in our lives."

The truth is, Alayna is a very good person, a very strong person and, I would even go so far as to say, a very righteous person. I've got a few more shades of gray than she has, which I think is one of the reasons God brought us together in the first place. That's also what the poem is about: how God put each in the other's life because He knew the contrast between us would work.

His purpose for our lives is a reflection of His presence in our lives. He loves us unconditionally, even though He is perfect and we're imperfect. In a marriage there has to be the same kind of unconditional love because, sooner or later, you're going to discover each other's imperfections. You're going to find major differences between each other, but if you're committed, you'll also discover that an amazing amount of love has been set aside for the two of you to work it out. Marriage is a picture of God's commitment to you, a model of how He is in it for the long haul, for richer or poorer, in sickness and in health. It's a simple message, but you can never hear it enough.

We hear a lot of talk about compatibility in marriage, but I think the marriages that work the best are the ones where the partners have very different sets of strengths and weaknesses. I'm able to accept the things that Alayna tells me about myself because she has respect and deep love for me, and I also know that God has put this very even-keeled, logical, and grounded person in my life because these are exactly the qualities I lack. That love between us comes into play when we're dealing with the brass-tacks issues of our relationship. It brings down the walls of defensiveness and allows each of us to really hear what the other is saying, regardless of how much it may make us uncomfortable to hear it. Alayna wants to see me become a better person, as I do for her. I feel myself completed when I'm with my wife, and she feels the same way with me.

The Divine Comedy

As this song proves, I consider myself as much a poet as I do a musician or a songwriter, even though I know that, these days, a poet doesn't have much chance of being heard beyond a small circle of friends. I think that's a shame. There were eras in history when the voices of poets spoke for entire cultures and societies, creating ways of seeing the world that still resonate today if we'd only take time to study them.

Art of any description needs support to survive, and there was once a time when the church most actively nurtured the artists in its midst. From the inspired music of Bach and Brahms to the paintings and sculptures of Michelangelo to *The Divine Comedy* of Dante, the church has been the repository of the greatest masterpieces of the Christian world, and that's a relationship I pray will be restored one day. It's not just that art makes for good evangelism. It's that art is an expression of man's creativity, which, in turn, is a gift from God. As such, it should be celebrated for its own sake.

In dc Talk we have tried to create music that stands on its own yet also carries a message. As a result, I think God has used dc Talk in unique ways. I don't know of too many Christian bands that can appeal to a mass audience in the way we do. We can go into a completely mainstream environment and do a show, and the people will relate at least to the music—and, I hope, to the message behind the music.

It's hard in this culture to get people to focus long enough to actually hear what I'm saying. I do consider myself a poet, but poetry isn't exactly a means of mass communication, so I also work within a musical context. Ideally, however, poetry and music should be able to function separately. They are two different ways of communicating, and each is valid. The fact is, every artist has to work within the confines of the times in which he's living, and in these times it's easier to be heard through a song than through words on a page.

I actually wrote a book of poetry a few years ago, which I'm making available now over the Internet. I really appreciate an artist like Jewel, who uses her platform as a pop singer to expose her fans to her poetry. We should be able to express ourselves in a variety of forms. Paul McCartney paints. Sting is an actor. The reality is, no one is just one thing, and being pigeonholed into one aspect of talents and abilities is as much a trap as being told we don't have any talents or abilities whatsoever.

Sometimes people come up to me when I'm backstage or just walking down the street and ask me how they can break into the music business, be a songwriter, or get their demo heard. I try to be encouraging, but the first thing I want to tell them is to make sure they've really got what it takes to be an artist—not just to create, but to support themselves and their families through their creations.

If you think you want to be an artist, you have to be open to the fact that maybe God has something else in mind for you. Look at the pattern of your life. Has the urge to create been with you from the beginning? Has it been part of your life's journey from grade school to college and beyond?

"How are we going to spend the time God has given us on this earth? Where is our treasure, and what is our reward?"

I have friends in sales who are truly gifted in that area, and they realized at a certain point in their lives that they had a real talent for the job. They went to school and studied business and pursued a career in that world, and they're among the happiest and most fulfilled people I know. There are others who are gifted in bringing crops from the ground. They understand the seasons and the growing cycles, and they have a deep love for the earth. Their gift carries with it beauty and simplicity, too, just as there is anytime someone realizes what God has called him to do in life.

If we look at it carefully, almost all human activity is creative in one way or another. Creativity is building a house for the family. Creativity is raising children. Creativity is a very big concept, and it's not just about writing or singing songs.

The sad truth is, too many people are unhappy because they're seeking the wrong dream, and when it doesn't work out for them, they give up and opt out for some easy alternative. Too many people are just getting by. Although my heart goes out to them, I sometimes want to push them forward to strive for excellence, to give them the encouragement to take the next step.

I'm not just talking about homeless people or the dregs of society, either. I'm convinced that some individuals who are living highly successful lives with lots of outward signs of achievement go to bed at night feeling that something is missing, some piece of the puzzle. This life is very short, seventy or eighty years for most of us. How are we going to spend the time God has given us on this earth? Where is our treasure, and what is our reward?

We've all read books and seen TV programs about people who have had near-death experiences. What's interesting about those accounts is that those experiences have changed the lives of the people involved. Atheists on their deathbeds became convinced that there is a God. People who lived selfish lives repented and dedicated themselves to helping others.

Getting a glimpse behind the curtain to see eternity rocked their world.

It rocks mine; that's for sure. A few friends have died before their time, and I never felt prepared to deal with the reality of death and its implications for my time on earth. I had to acknowledge that there are bigger and more mysterious purposes to God's plan than I could ever comprehend. Life is unpredictable. That's the beauty of it. You just can't take it for granted.

*Alayna bought me my first puppy in Nashville,
an Irish wolfhound named Tully.*

Track
Eight

THE SECRET CIRCLE

Oh tell me, do you live in dreams?
You're not exactly what you seem to be
Yeah, we want to follow Ellesun
But come tomorrow we will want to run from Ellesun
Oh no

You're so fashionably late
And you're wearing all that black like fate
You wanna run to the forest all the time

She's got a ring of serpents
One red, one green, entwined
She's got skeletons in her closet
That always seems to fall in line

I wonder if she's lost it in the head
Yeah, she just wants to get you into bad
Just take another prisoner, Ellesun
Oh yeah, just tell another lie until it's done
Oh my

Your name cannot be traced
And your theology is out of date
You wanna run to the fairies all the time

She offers you the ring of serpents
And she offers you her hand
It's not like love or friendship
It's something hidden

Oh the meeting's on, it's such a secret circle
Secret circle of, secret circle of, secret circle of . . .

Oh tell me, do you live in dreams?
You're not exactly what you seem to be
Ellesun

Written by Kevin Max and Erick Cole. © 2001 Blind Thief Publishing (BMI) (admin. by EMI CMP) / Songs from the Playground (ASCAP) (admin. by Franklin Mgmt. Group, Inc.).

THE SECRET CIRCLE

"The Secret Circle" is a tough song for me to talk about because it's based on a real experience. I was hanging out with some of those fringe people I was drawn to at that period of my life. I assumed they were more or less normal and well-adjusted and were just a little rebellious and looking to kick up their heels. That is, until one day when I discovered that they were involved in some very dark stuff—things I don't want to go into here. Suffice it to say, it shook me up pretty good. I was angry and confused, and I broke those ties quickly and completely.

Later, I realized they had probably gotten mixed up in things that were way over their heads. I didn't know what to do for them at the time except pray, and it was only years later that I was able to think clearly enough about that time in my life to write a song about it.

A Walk on the Dark Side

My close encounter with darkness left a mark on me, so much so that when I started writing this song, I wasn't immediately conscious that I had chosen the experience as my subject. I had finished the music and recorded the track without lyrics, and when I started writing them down, I had the strange sensation that I was trying to shake something loose in my head. Up until that point I think I had buried the memory.

The memory is more than a little haunting, but if you asked me whether I thought those kids were actually in a league with Satan, I couldn't honestly say for sure. Maybe they were just trying to freak people out. Like many people at that age, they also probably had a lot of things rolling around in their heads all at once, things that might be hard to sort out without the wisdom and guidance of someone they could trust and believe in. I wish I could have been that person, but I was pretty mixed up myself back then. All I can say for sure was that the experience frightened me. It wasn't as if I had to make up my mind. Like I said earlier, I turned and ran as fast as I could, out of pure instinct.

The Reality of Evil

Since then I've done a little studying about all kinds of evil, including satanism, and I've discovered that it's a cult that actively tries to recruit people. There are different denominations of the satanic church, just as there are different denominations of Christianity, and some of the major denominations don't believe in an actual devil. Their philosophy can be summed up as humanism, the belief that man is totally free to create his own reality and live by his own code of behavior. Man can do whatever he wants to do without worrying about the consequences. Man is the deity, and because he is, he is the ultimate authority, answerable only to his own ambitions and desires. There's no deity of Satan to worship. Man worships himself.

> "I believe 100 percent in spiritual forces of evil and the reality of demon possession."

To me, that's a much more insidious evil than a bunch of people in black robes playing around with skulls and candles. Putting man in the place of God is a sin that's much less showy but much more damaging.

I believe 100 percent in spiritual forces of evil and the reality of demon possession. First Peter 5:8 warns us, "Be on the alert. Your adversary, the devil, prowls around like a roaring lion, seeking someone to devour." I have personally known people that I consider to have been demon possessed, and I have seen firsthand all the characteristics of demon possession. It's completely real and should be taken very seriously.

Real wisdom lies in knowing what we're dealing with, and whether the forces allied against God are overt or incognito, we need to be aware of their wiles and strategies. Demonic possession, in my opinion, is easy enough to spot, and it happens when a person leaves himself open to that experience.

But demons use and abuse people in other ways as well. There's a battle going on all around us, and we take casualties, just as there are in any war. Anyone who dismisses the concept of angelic beings, good or evil, is leaving himself wide open to deception and oppression. I studied the subject of angels quite a bit, and on both sides of the battle lines there are hierarchies and ranks of spiritual beings. There are guardian angels and messenger angels and warrior angels, and ranks of angels who spend eternity just worshiping and praising God. That's their job, and for every heavenly being there is a satanic counterpart.

Look around. Open your eyes. We're in the midst of spiritual warfare, and we can see the ebb and flow of the battle in everyday life if we can read the signs of the times.

I acknowledge the reality of demonic realms, but I also happen to believe that a demon cannot possess a believer, someone in whom the Spirit of God is dwelling. When you're saved, that Spirit comes to live inside you, and nothing can dislodge Him. Demons may try to torment you and make your life miserable, but when they come up against the blinding light of the Holy Spirit, they're helpless to act.

Being shielded in that way doesn't give us license to be foolhardy, though. Have you ever been in certain places where you've felt a strong spiritual vibe, or you've been with a person who radiates a powerful presence, for good or evil? I have. There are those who are gifted to be more in touch with those realms, but I think it's within everyone's capacity to be spiritually discerning. We hear things and see things and experience things all the time that give us clues about what's happening in the invisible realms. It's up to us to cultivate that sixth sense.

Serving Yourself

My strange encounter with darkness taught me a lot. I had the scary conviction that I had opened myself up to powerful forces beyond my control and had risked throwing away my beliefs for a moment of passing pleasure. I didn't let many people know at that time what I had learned, but I did pray a lot, asking God for protection.

I considered it a lesson to be learned; I needed to know people a little bit better before going deeper into a relationship with them. I could use the excuse that when I was in college and away from my parents for the first time in my life, I was experiencing things and meeting people, and maybe my defenses were down. I was learning as I went. But the truth is, sometimes the lessons we're meant to learn come too late to do us any good.

In telling this story, even in very indirect terms, I realize I run the risk of disapproval from the Christian community. There's nothing I can do about that. I'm trying to be honest about myself and my life, warts and all, and I think the fear that someone like me is going to influence somebody else to do the same things I did shows a real lack of faith in each other. People can make up their own minds. They can form their own judgments and exercise their own free will.

If I'm going to influence anybody, I hope it would be to help you think for yourself. I can't live your life for you, even though I hope my example can help you to avoid some of my slipups. But the bottom line is, you'll make your own mistakes, draw your own conclusions, and try to do it better the next time. God has given you the freedom to go for it. Don't let Him down.

Although "The Secret Circle" is about a real-life experience, the song can be taken from several different points of view. It can be about a disillusioned person or somebody who's manipulative and controlling. It has a Gothic feel to it, and you may appreciate it only on a musical level. That's up to you. The point I wanted to make is really very simple and straightforward: run from evil; run from things that will drag you down. At the most basic level, it's an account of one man's experience, brushing up against the dark side and finding that if you go too far, you can get burned.

> "We live in a time when evil has more of an appeal than what is true and good and constructive."

Take it for what it's worth. Play on the fringes with fringe people and dabble in darkness at your own risk. We live in a time when evil has more of an appeal than what is true and good and constructive. Why that's true is a mystery to me, and I'm drawn to the mysteries of life, but I've come the hard way to the conclusion that serving the dark side is ultimately just serving yourself. Evil is about choosing your own desires and not caring about anyone else. It's about exalting yourself above God. And pretty soon you just don't care anymore. And that's when you're really in danger.

Kmax in France during writers' week at Miles Copeland's house

Track Nine

I DON'T BELONG

And so we broke up
And so you decided
It was you, it's always you
Even though we were friends
I felt uninvited
The fraternity of fools

And I'm drowning slowly (going down)
And I'm fading like ink that's a hundred years old

Chorus
I don't belong, say I'm wrong
Told you that you should have known me better
I don't belong, this is my song, this is my song

You made me a prince
You made me a pauper
Then you turned and closed the gate
Even though I messed up
There wasn't an offer, love
No mercy, no grace

And I see right through you (see right through you)
You wanna be just like me, don't you?

Chorus

(stupid things I've said and done)
Oh don't you walk away
(battles that I've lost and won)
Shame, shame, shame on me
(what I used to think was wrong)
I'm for the underdog, I like the one that don't belong

Chorus

Written by Kevin Max and Owsley. © 2001 Blind Thief Publishing (BMI)
(admin. by EMI CMP).

I DON'T BELONG

"I Don't Belong" is a song written about a specific feeling I've had for some time that I'm really a misfit in the Christian music community. Even in dc Talk, over the past three or four years, I've had the growing conviction that I didn't fit in. It's not that I've been persecuted or excluded, even though I have had my run-ins with the powers that be. It's just that with many of the relationships I've formed, there's been an assumption that I agree with positions that have been taken and decisions that have been made, and that has not necessarily been the case. Christians sometimes think that every believer thinks as they do, without taking the time to understand the individual and what makes him tick.

As a result, I've often retreated within myself, doing what was expected of me, the way it was supposed to be done, but without conviction or commitment. I knew in my heart that there were aspects of being in the role of a spokesperson that made me uncomfortable and that, even musically, there were different approaches I would have liked to take.

I have very definite ideas and strong opinions. That's just the way I'm made, and I've been put into a collaborative part-nership with two other guys who also have their own way of doing things. There has to be compromise, which I don't object to, except that, as time went on, I increasingly wanted to spread my wings and fly on my own. I think that's a normal feeling and one that comes from holding back personal convictions for the sake of a collective goal.

> *"Christians sometimes think that every believer thinks as they do, without taking the time to understand the individual and what makes him tick."*

Within dc Talk, Toby and Mike are very similar in their personalities and the way they approach music. More often than not, I've been the third wheel, but I've never wavered in my belief that creatively the group's success has always been the result of three individual talents working together.

On the Payroll

In a very real way I have the same feeling about Christian music as a whole. What excites me and inspires me sometimes seems to be very different from what is considered acceptable within that industry. For a long time I've wanted to expand the horizons of Christian music, open it up to more diverse expressions of faith, and let different kinds of music have a chance to be heard. Being part of a community is a great thing and necessary if we're going to accomplish important goals. But ultimately it's the individual that counts. God doesn't know us by our labels; He knows each of us by name.

It's the feeling of being on the outside looking in that I wanted to express in this song. A friend of mine, the recording artist Owsley, encouraged me to identify those emotions and helped me put them into words and music. The song started out from a personal point of view, about how it felt being at the peak of the Christian music world but not wholeheartedly endorsing everything that goes on within that world. But as I continued to write, it became more and more about my situation within dc Talk.

Some of our fans may be surprised to hear that we actively considered breaking up at a certain point. My sense of alienation had become very acute, and although I know that Toby and Mike understood the way I was feeling, it seemed that I was trapped in the business. To put it bluntly, I'd lost touch with the reason I'd joined in the first place—because I love to sing and write and perform. It was a job, and many people on the dc Talk payroll were depending on me to do that job.

I was boxed in, trapped in a creative and commercial prison that kept me from expressing who I really was. I'm convinced that our audience has always been behind us, supporting our music and our mission, but there have been other elements, very conservative and legalistic elements, within the Christian community that couldn't accept someone who colored outside the lines.

Sometimes, for example, I'd get a little carried away onstage, throw water out on the audience, tell a joke, or do a dance move that some people considered suggestive. I've done some things just to be provocative. My intent was never to offend anyone, however. I don't deliberately try to shock people. But if in my enthusiasm I end up doing things that are considered to be crossing some invisible line and I upset people who don't want to experience anything outside a prescribed behavior, then I've got to wonder who has the problem. Those people or yours truly? Ultimately I want to take as much responsibility as is rightfully mine. There are such things as words and actions that are permissible but not profitable, and perhaps I have gone too far on occasion.

> "I refuse to go quietly into some musical ghetto just because I happen to believe in Jesus."

The truth is, there are more opportunities to be an effective artist and a committed Christian than what is offered only in the realm known as Christian music. There are better ways of reaching the members of an audience than preaching at them, no matter how good the music is that's backing up the sermon. The whole idea of a music genre called "Christian rock" is based on a false premise. Rock and roll was born in the church, and anyone who has gone to a full-on black gospel service knows it's true. Sure, there's praise and worship music, but in its essence the sounds of celebration that are the roots of rock and roll were nurtured in the choir loft.

Let's take back what belonged to us in the first place. I refuse to go quietly into some musical ghetto just because I happen to believe in Jesus. We have a powerful and life-changing message to bring to the world. We don't need a different brand of music to make it acceptable. Maybe record label executives and radio station music directors don't want us singing about God. They'd rather have us shunted off into little slices of the airwaves or some bin in the back of the store

Typical Kevin Max behavior problem

where others of "our kind" can be herded together and mar-
ginalized and sold a lot of mediocre products that have been
packaged to appeal to our "demographic."

Barnstorming for God

From the beginning dc Talk tried to break out of that
bondage, and *Jesus Freak* was the first time we succeeded. That
album really blew down the doors. It won a Grammy, sold two
million records, and got three and a half out of four stars in a
Rolling Stone magazine review. It was a critical hit and a commercial smash. Even more important, it was a consistent piece
of art, not just for Christians, but across the board.

We went out of our way to make aggressive, cutting-edge
videos, and we pushed the envelope in every other way we
could think of. Sure, we wanted to attract attention. We
wanted to make some noise. It was time for Christians to make
a stand, and there was no stopping us. Then we did it all over
again with *Supernatural*, creating a concert experience that
could stand up to anything anyone else was putting onstage.

I've heard it said that we were unlike anything that had
come before or since, a musical force unto ourselves. But with
success came new challenges, and the differences of opinion
and approach began to become more apparent within the
group. Toby's heartfelt desire was to write blatant, up-front
songs with the clear intent to evangelize the audience—"to
point them to the truth," as he has stated. Mike, acting out of
his own convictions, lined up with Toby, while I was inter-

ested in pursuing another approach entirely, one that was more subtle and personal. I was really pushing to get our music out into the mainstream, trying to find a way to bring more people in.

The tensions began to show. There were those in the dc Talk organization who were very vocal about their concern for keeping the base happy, holding on to the fans we'd already acquired, and not risking things that would alienate the mass marketers of Christian products. The whole conflict came to a head for me toward the end of the *Supernatural* tour. I had begun to rebel and want to push the envelope offstage as well as on. I was looking for an "out," because I felt I was bouncing off the ceiling of the CCM world. I suddenly announced that I needed to do something on my own. I was going to fulfill my obligations, of course, but as soon as I could free myself up, I was determined to create a musical expression that was purely from my heart and my head.

If you listen closely, you can hear that determination in "I Don't Belong." When I wrote the song with Owsley, I was going through a whole gamut of emotions, feeling disillusioned and let down. But even in the midst of all that, toward the end of the song, I began to see my way clear toward a new attitude: "(stupid things I've said and done) / Oh don't you walk away / (battles that I've lost and won) / Shame, shame, shame on me."

I think writing this song helped me come full circle in my relationship with Toby and Mike and see the future of dc Talk in a different light. I realized that it was important for me to be willing to work out my problems with the guys. We were a band with a very special purpose to our music, and we'd all worked hard over the years to bring that purpose to fruition. We didn't totally agree on every creative and commercial point, but we did agree on one thing: we wanted to reach as many people as possible with as uplifting and positive a message as possible. And we're going to continue to do that as dc Talk.

So what about my own goals and ambitions? What about the KMax sound? Well, the simple answer is, I can do both. I'm not interested in taking baby steps. With this record, I'm jumping in with both feet. This isn't just a side project from the lead singer of the Christian rock supergroup dc Talk. I'm a brand-new artist, and this is a brand-new day.

Playing boccie at Toby's house

I've been able to use what I've learned by being in the circumstances described in "I Don't Belong" in my personal and professional growth. Okay, so I'm a bit of a freak. Okay, so I don't really fit in. Maybe I'll be ostracized by most of society when they find out I'm a Christian. And maybe I'll be ostracized by Christians when they find out I want to have an impact on society. If that's the price I have to pay for being myself, bring it on.

Ultimately the message of "I Don't Belong" is about learning to respect each other. It's something we had to learn to do in dc Talk, something we neglected in the early days. But that's changed, and when we get back together to do another record, it's going to be based on mutual respect. We really feel like a team now, and as a team, we can do anything, up to and including making room for each other.

People ask me what will happen to dc Talk if my solo record becomes a big success or if Toby or Mike makes a solo record that really takes off. I can't say for sure. But I do know one thing. Whether dc Talk makes one more album or ten more albums, we'll always be a family. And families stick together.

And I believe our fans, like a family, will stick by us. The people who go to our concerts and buy our records—probably some of the same ones who are reading this book—have given dc Talk an incredible opportunity to speak God's truth to the world. I want to make sure to thank them every opportunity I get, so, from the bottom of my heart, thanks.

Kevin and his father, Max Smith

Track Ten

BLIND

There's no one stirring on my street tonight
There's no one leaning on my windowpane
No one to ascertain, or just apologize to
There's no one to kill my anxiousness again

And if you can, please take these arrows from my side
Their poison marks are like a tattoo of my pride
I'm guilty, so guilty, dead guilty

Blind, I'm blind
You know I'm blind, baby, say it isn't right
So blind, I'm blind
I'm certifiable but I'm on time

No priest in midnight black can cure my itching flea
This case of stricken lust has really got a hold on me

And if you can, please take this sword back
    from my side
Its poison mark is like a tattoo of my pride
I'm guilty, so shoot me, I'm guilty

Blind, I'm blind
You know I'm losing my mind, I'm paralyzed
So blind, I'm blind
Certifiable but right in time

Wooo hooo, wooo hooo
I need divine intervention, Your divine intervention
You're divine, You're the vine,
I'm the branch, You're the vine,
I'm the fig leaf, You're the branch, You're divine

I'm blind (I'm deaf and dumb and that's not all)
You know I need a dose of Your spirituality
I'm blind (I'm deaf and dumb and that's not all)
I can see now my eyes are opening
I'm deaf and dumb and that's not all
I'm deaf and dumb to it all

Written by Kevin Max and Erick Cole. © 2001 Blind Thief Publishing (BMI)
(admin. by EMI CMP) / Songs from the Playground (ASCAP) (admin. by Franklin Mgmt.
Group, Inc.).

"Blind" is based on some of my experiences during my single days and my need back then to always be accepted. I wanted to find someone who would take me just as I was, without requiring any changes on my part, and I inevitably found myself disappointed when it didn't turn out that way.

The song also deals with what I'd call the phenomenon of spontaneous physical combustion that comes as a result of acting on impulse and not really thinking through the consequences of a relationship. It's a sin with roots in the basic tug-of-war between the flesh and the spirit. I wanted to capture the feeling that comes after giving in to lust and temptation, the emptiness and guilt that can sometimes be completely overwhelming—far more so than any transitory enjoyment that might be experienced.

"I'm blind . . . I'm deaf and dumb to it all." That refrain is trying to describe the numb feeling that comes over me when

I know I'm doing something that is at war with my conscience, but I go ahead and do it anyway, just to find out what it would be like.

It's an experience that I was very familiar with during one period of my life, a time when I was maybe a little overly impressed by good-looking women and, as a result, developed an appetite for variety that was driving me from one unhealthy and unsatisfactory infatuation to the next. Looking back, I can see that I never wanted to be locked into anything serious and what I was really looking for was not so much a physical connection, but the crying need for a woman to accept me, to make me feel important. I think a lot of us guys feel inadequate without a female building us up and stroking our egos. There was a season in my life when I sought that out, and I became very needy without really knowing what I needed.

The Fishbowl

It was a time when I was constantly on the road, performing in one city after another, night after night, until everything was a big blur. Anyone who's ever been in that situation can tell you how fast and completely you lose touch with reality. So much so that when I'd finish up a tour and get back home, I would immediately start looking for the same kind of intense, exciting, and temporary relationships that were so common on the road.

But even as I was looking for a connection, I would keep those women at arm's length, never letting them see inside me. When I sat down to write this song, I had in mind that impoverished condition—the hunger for acceptance that led me to give in to temptation because of my lack of emotional and spiritual depth. The physical connection was sparked by the need to be built up, not anything I was willing to put back into the relationship. I was taking, not giving, and even if sometimes it was more of a mental link than a sexual one, it didn't really matter. I had no idea how to establish commitment and respect.

Living life in a celebrity fishbowl, even within the Christian music world, makes it all too easy to lose touch with personal values. I think, deep down inside, that I knew the difference between a one-night stand on the road and the possibility of a real and lasting relationship. As a consequence, I was always guarded with the people I met on tour and a little bit more myself when I got home. The problem was, those two aspects of my personality were getting more and more intermingled until I wasn't exactly sure who I was or how to act around people who wanted to get next to me.

As I mentioned before, the Christian rock scene has its share of people who are attracted to the bright lights of celebrity, and some girls I met on the road with dc Talk could definitely be construed as groupies. But what fascinated me, especially in the early days of the band, was how many mothers would show up backstage and try to push their daughters at me, insisting that I date their girls as if I were the only eligible bachelor in a hundred-mile radius. Of course, I was confronted with the usual assortment of freaks who would come out of the woodwork anywhere I went, along with the occasional brazen fan who would press her hotel key into the palm of my hand. Maybe it didn't happen as frequently or as blatantly as in the mainstream rock and roll world, but anyone who was looking for that kind of interaction could find it.

The majority of our audience was made up of girls, particularly when we were first starting out, and there was always the temptation to try to cash in on our growing celebrity. But I think the three of us realized very early that succumbing to the loneliness and isolation that come from constantly being on the road could be very destructive to our careers and reputations. Ultimately, the prospect of letting each other down provided a strong incentive to stay out of trouble. In a very important way, we kept each other accountable.

But the problems really began after I got off the road. When I could finally just be me, I discovered that I didn't know who *me* was. I've always believed that the mark of a true musical professional is that, when he gets off the stage, he is able to take off his rock star mask and resume a normal life. It's an issue I've struggled with, and there's no question that, through my marriage and the process of maturing, I'm much better able to distinguish between what is real and what isn't.

Getting in Touch with the Feminine Side

Once again, the quality of humility is invaluable—knowing who we are, the good and the bad, and understanding that there is more to life than just our own selfish needs. It's a process that happens over time, living each day as it comes and being open to the wisdom that experience bestows. But I wouldn't say that it comes to us naturally. Humility is a gift from God, and as imperfect humans, we try everything we can think of to reject that gift. I never wanted to admit, to myself or anyone else, that I had an uncontrollable need to feel wanted and loved.

Maybe it stemmed from the fact that I had been given away as an infant and never really knew my birth mother. My adoptive mother was a wonderful woman,

> "Humility is a gift from God, and as imperfect humans, we try everything we can think of to reject that gift."

a great example of a godly female presence in my life, but there always seemed to be a question mark left hanging: Who was my real mother? What role would she have played in my life if things had turned out differently?

But it could also have been an unavoidable result of my chosen profession. Because I am a performer, people were always telling me how my music had affected them, how much I meant to them, and how they admired me as a role model and even as a spiritual teacher. Then when I was out of the limelight and didn't have people tickling my ears, maybe I wanted to go out and look for attention.

Actually I think the truth is much simpler than either scenario. I've always loved women and their perspective on life, and I've always had a better time hanging out with girls than with guys. There's just something about the female mind that draws me, that makes me feel free to be vulnerable and real about myself and my hopes and fears. Being around a woman gives me a sense of security, and to my way of thinking, there's nothing wrong with that. It's healthy for a man and a woman to find contentment and fulfillment in each other.

The problem for me was that I didn't know how to give back what was needed for *them* to feel secure and valued as individuals. And that was exactly when those relationships started to backfire on me. The stronger women would come right out and tell me, front and center, that they expected more than what I was giving, and when that happened, I'd jump ship and look for someone who would better meet my needs without making any demands of her own. Then we'd have fun for a while before the whole process started up again.

I guess I shouldn't have been surprised when I started hearing around town that I was getting a reputation. I'd never set out to hurt anybody. I'm not that kind of person. In fact, I'm just the opposite. I want people to feel comfortable and at ease when they're around me. But because of the sheer number of relationships I was having, and the quick turnaround time, I was starting to make people angry with me and suspicious of my motives.

And when I caught wind of that, I decided I needed to go through a period of time when I wasn't seeing anybody. I realized I had to get a grip and focus on the real problems that were confronting me and the real solutions that I knew were available. I made a conscious decision to pray to God to help me discover what I was seeking and, even more than that, to involve Him in the situation directly.

The reality I finally had to face was that for a long time I had been out on the edge spiritually. I had fooled myself into thinking I was maintaining a Christian lifestyle, but that was a self-serving deception. I had to get back to what I knew was right, the real source of security that I had somehow drifted away from. I was heading down a road that led to an abyss of never-ending hunger and needs that would never be answered.

Alayna

It's pretty ironic, in retrospect, because right around that time dc Talk was starting to meet with substantial success in the realm of Christian rock music. I should have been sitting on top of the world. But think about it. Give somebody an enormous amount of attention and acclaim, couple that with a lot of money and no responsibilities or accountability, and what you've done is set him up to fall right off the edge. Some people have never been able to crawl back. I was different. I cried out to God, and He led me to safety and restored me to a close and intimate relationship with Him and with the wife that He brought into my life.

Because of those prayers, I'm convinced, because I diligently and earnestly asked for God's help, He brought me Alayna. From the very beginning, ours was different from any other relationship I'd ever had with a woman. First of all,

"The Tin Angel" performance at Nashville Summer Stages

before we got seriously involved, we developed a friendship, and that was a major shift in priorities for me. I would tell anyone contemplating a long-term relationship to follow this simple rule: make sure you can be friends with the person before you move on to more serious things. Friendship is the basis of everything else that will follow, and without that foundation, you might as well not waste each other's time. All together, Alayna and I dated almost two years, and there was another year when we didn't see each other at all before we finally got together for good.

That was a real change of pace for me. At that time I met and dated so many girls, I couldn't keep track of them any longer. The guys in the band used to joke that, wherever I was, I would put out my antenna and send up my girl-finding satellite. But with Alayna it was different. She wanted to take it slow, and for the first time in my life, so did I. I wasn't sure where we were heading, but I think I knew deep down inside that it was going to be something special. To tell you the truth, that freaked me out.

We saw each other exclusively for about a year. Then for about six months things got very serious, at which point I became frightened of the whole idea of commitment. That was the first time that I had been in a really rooted and firmly established relationship with somebody who truly knew me and saw behind the rock star mask to all my faults—and loved me just the same. I had found somebody who could give me what I had been looking for so long and hard, but instead of embracing her, I ran far and fast.

It all came to a head during the end of the *Jesus Freak* tour when we started playing concerts overseas, basically touring the world. Once again, I was putting out my antenna, looking for something that I already had and sliding back into my old ways. I ended up alone in Spain after the tour was over. The rest of the group had gone home, but I'd decided to stay in Europe because I'd met a girl in Holland after one of our shows and she gave me her number in Spain.

We spent a weekend hanging out together, traveling through Spain and Portugal. Right in the middle of the idyllic escape from reality, I had the overwhelming conviction that I wanted to be with Alayna. It really had nothing to do with this girl, who was a very nice person, but I sat her down one evening and said, "You know what? I'm moving farther and

farther away from something I had that was very real, and I've
got to try to get back, to retrace my steps to the last place I
know that I really belonged." I called Alayna that night. Two
days later I was back home, and two weeks after that we were
engaged to be married.

Alayna is a musician and a songwriter, too, and when I pro-
posed to her, she was onstage doing a show. I came out from
behind the curtain, and she had no clue about what I was
going to do. When I asked her to marry me, she looked to her
twin sister, who was performing with her, as if asking for guidance, and her sister gave her a nod. Right there, in front of
about 150 people in that little bar, she said yes.

Step by Step

I later found out that the year during which we were sepa-
rated was one of the most difficult times in Alayna's life. It was
all the more devastating because she was convinced that we
were meant to be together, even when I was fighting the whole
idea of making a commitment. It was the first time that she
had really fallen in love, the first time for both of us. When it
started breaking down, she couldn't help wondering what she
had done wrong.

As for me, I had a deep feeling of shame over my behavior
that I tried to hide from myself and everyone else. I considered
myself unworthy of her. I thought she was too intensely good
to want to deal with me anymore. I put her on a pedestal in
my mind, which was really just another way of avoiding my

fear about giving myself totally to one person. I had tried to
rationalize it away, telling myself there was just no way that
this woman would want to spend the rest of her life with me.

I was too irresponsible, too way-
ward, too scattered. And you
know what? I was all of those
things and more. But she didn't
let that stop her. Step by step,
day by day, we learned how to
make it work, depending on
each other, learning from each
other, and trusting God to get
us over the rough spots.

> "I believe that the Spirit
> of God was constantly
> guiding me, even in my
> backslidden condition,
> living on the outskirts
> of my Christianity."

I sometimes wonder whether I could truly comprehend
how blessed I am to have found Alayna if I hadn't had to go
through everything I did to get to her in the first place. The
answer, I think, goes back to each person being who he is and
learning the lessons life has to teach him.

For some of us, life is a journey on a very twisting road. We
don't learn right away. We don't find the answers in a flash
of insight. Others understand what's important instinctively.
They are more rooted, not so restless and driven.

Speaking personally, I had to go on that journey to find out
where my threshold was. I believe that I did have to make
those mistakes to find out what Alayna truly meant to me.
Maybe there was an easier way, but if there was, maybe I
wouldn't have chosen it. I believe that the Spirit of God was
constantly guiding me, even in my backslidden condition,

living on the outskirts of my Christianity. I was like a blind bat, flying from steeple to steeple, looking for a place to hide, but being pulled in by a tractor beam the whole time. God was there throughout the whole process, waiting for me to look back over my shoulder and see my need for Him.

Who knows what would have happened if I hadn't been convicted of my sin and started to pray? When we invite God into a scenario, the truth is revealed. We may have to go through a lot of weirdness, but it's all for a reason. We're not going to get the answers we seek unless we ask. Making mistakes is one of the ways we ask. We don't need to be sinners to learn about God's love, but the truth is that we are, and God still loves us.

Track Eleven

ON AND ON

You are the sunshine
I am the rain that falls in line
You are a candle
And I am your darkness
You are the moonlight
I am the cloud that passes by
You are a vision
And I am blindness

And so it goes
The story is far too old to know it all

Chorus
On and on, we dance until the song is off the radio
On and on, we hold each other long after
    the crowd is gone
On and on, our love goes on and on

You are an island
I am the raging of the sea
You are a fortress
And I am abandoned
You are the valley
You are the bird that flies so high
You are a temple
And I am a beggar

And so it goes
The story is far too old to know it all

Chorus

Take me to your drawbridge, come take me to your door
Take me when I'm hungry, baby, take me when I'm poor
Take me when I'm sick of love, take me when
    you've had enough
Take me when I'm lost, alone, and don't know
    the reasons why

Written by Kevin Max and Erick Cole. © 2001 Blind Thief Publishing (BMI)
(admin. by EMI CMP) / Sad Astronaught Music (BMI).

"On and On" is a song for and about my wife. It came into being at the eleventh hour, with Alayna prompting me to write a ballad, so I guess she's responsible for it in that way as well.

I'm not really big on ballads, but she told me she felt that the record needed one to balance out some of the more up-tempo material. I said, "Well, you go write one then, because I'm no good at it." We went round and round, and I finally agreed to give it a try. I literally wrote "On and On" in one night. I don't think there's any mystery about what it means: this is how I feel about Alayna.

In every sense she completes me, but there's also a part of me, deep inside, that still carries baggage from the past and that's something she's been willing to live with and try to heal. I'm profoundly grateful to her for that, which is also an important part of this ballad: "You are a candle / And I am your darkness." There are times when I can be overpowering and very difficult to live with, and in the song I face up to that and ask her to help me be a better person:

> Take me to your drawbridge, come take me to your door
> Take me when I'm hungry, baby, take me when I'm poor
> Take me when I'm sick of love, take me when you've had
>   enough

To me, that's a perfect picture of marriage, a commitment for better or for worse. In "On and On" I think I paint a picture of our relationship that's a little more dramatic than it is in reality. Alayna has weaknesses like anyone else, and I'm not that total basket case who's singing the song. In real life we even each other out more. But it's also absolutely true that we depend on each other for the unconditional love and acceptance that have to be present for any marriage to survive. As you've probably guessed, Alayna is the most significant person in my life.

The Tree in the House

She's originally from Houston, Texas, and grew up in a family with her twin sister, Audra, and another set of identical twins. Her parents divorced when she was twelve, and there are probably as many identity issues in that family situation as there were in mine. But Alayna is a very strong and assertive person who staked out her territory from the beginning. One of the ways that Alayna is different from me is that she's always had a solid sense of herself. Growing up in a large family, she had to figure out who she was right away, or somebody else would show her. She had to fend for herself quickly.

She's also quite talented musically. She and Audra started singing and playing music in high school and eventually went to Nashville to pursue a musical career. That is where we met. I always knew that I'd marry an artist because I'm drawn to people who are interested in creativity. Our musical tastes might be different, but we appreciate each other's work and are committed to excellence in our music.

> "To anyone who says that I need to be the *spiritual* leader in my marriage, I say that if we're not leading each other, we're in *trouble.*"

Alayna wasn't born into a Christian environment, but she started gravitating toward spirituality at a very young age. She and her sister came to the Lord through the writings of Francis Schaeffer.

Over the years she has come to express her faith differently from the way I do. She's not as much a restless seeker and a wandering spirit as I am. She's incredibly grounded and pragmatic and logical and all of the things that I'm not. You'd think that with such different personalities, there would be a lot of sparks flying, but that really hasn't happened. I think the common denominator of our faith has prevented that. We're very much on the same plane spiritually.

In Christian circles I know there's talk about how the man

is supposed to be the spiritual leader of the family, but I don't agree. It takes two people for it to work the way it should, and assuming that God speaks only to the man is just ludicrous. Sure, Scripture says that God created woman as a helpmate, but if a woman's mind and heart and spirit are open to God, He's going to work through them just as much as through any man. In fact, I think that spiritually women tend to be more open than men. They're more in tune, more open to what God is doing in any given situation. We're on the same playing field, and to anyone who says that I need to be the spiritual leader in my marriage, I say that if we're not leading each other, we're in trouble.

> "Some of us are living in a *romantic fantasy,* unwilling to acknowledge that *nobody's perfect* and that we all come with our own *price tags and baggage.*"

Writing "On and On" meant a lot to Alayna because, even though I may have exaggerated her virtues and my vices, she knows that I want our marriage to be as passionate and powerful as the best poetry. I try to live out my life like a poem, and so does she. We're artists, two hearts beating as one, which is why I can write my feelings without being shy or embarrassed. She knows how I feel about her. I wish every husband could feel the same about his wife.

I sometimes wonder if everyone in the world has someone who's meant for him, the way Alayna was meant for me. It's a perplexing question. I tend to be a positive thinker, and from

Above:
The bride's cake

'Til death
do us part

that viewpoint, I do believe that a partner is out there for everyone—a suitable partner, but maybe not a perfect one. Some of us are living in a romantic fantasy, unwilling to acknowledge that nobody's perfect and that we all come with our own price tags and baggage. Those people are setting themselves up for disillusionment.

C. S. Lewis offered some wonderful comments about marriage and the problems that inevitably arise. He compared it to a tree growing up through your house. On your way to the door you have to walk around the tree. You can't pretend that it doesn't exist or that it's not important. And sometimes you have to prune its branches or it will get out of control. It's a good analogy. If you don't catch problems early in a marriage, they will grow of their own accord and wreck your home. It takes a lot of tender loving care to grow a marriage and keep your house in one piece.

Over the years of my marriage, I've learned to cherish the qualities in Alayna that help me to be a better person. In many ways she has been a teacher to me, my personal *sensei*. She has taught me a lot about the social graces, when to shut up and when to speak up, and generally how to treat people. Through her example, she has taught me how to build friendships and nurture relationships. I used to be very closed, looking for what I could get out of people instead of what I could give.

Those changes didn't happen without conflict, of course. They say you can't teach an old dog new tricks, and I was a twenty-eight-year-old dog who had been doing it my way for a long time, so she and I had to work through my insecurities together. I also had to learn to accept her very direct and straightforward way of dealing with me. She wasn't inclined to coddle me or tolerate behavior that jeopardized the honest communication we were establishing. The fact is, while my wife can be very disarming, she'll tell you in a split second what she thinks, with no pretense. She's not loud or rude, but she cuts right to the chase.

A good example of her ability to speak the truth in love happened when I thought about leaving dc Talk. She was the one who opened my eyes to how blessed I was to be in a successful group, and she encouraged me to be thankful for the friendships that I have with Toby and Mike, to be respectful of the strong bonds we had built up over the years. Without her, I might have done something spontaneous that I probably would have regretted later.

Alayna and I complement each other, and to me, that's the miracle of our relationship. We're two very different people living under the same roof, each of whom has been given the exact set of personal characteristics necessary to be a friend, a teacher, and a companion to the other.

But it doesn't take being married to be able to serve each other in those ways. We can, and should, express the love of God in all our relationships. Marriage helps us understand the value of commitment, and so does being a friend to someone. It's all about laying down our lives for others.

On the road with friends

Track
Twelve

HER GAME

Every time she comes my way she knows just what
    to do and say
Those little smiles she throws away, they turn
    my stomach
If you listen close enough you'll catch all the
    divisive stuff
Those subtle moves, the way she smooths her hair

And you don't want to say
She was digging your grave
And your friends all can see it
There's no way you're gonna leave it

So where you gonna go,
Who you gonna call
When you know it's time to play the game?
What's your mystery,
Who's it gonna be
When you know it's time to play her game?

Chorus
Is it real or Memorex
Those secrets that you feared confess
When she was there you let it all spill out
Turning as you leave for good
You wonder if you ever should have wandered through
Her neighborhood at all

And you don't want to say
She was digging your grave
And your friends all can see it
There's no way you're gonna leave it

Chorus

I am all to blame
This is my parade of broken-hearted words
I feel them all and learned their shame
Please catch me when I fall
And turn me from this wall I've faced for far too long
This lonely sonnet needs a throng

HER GAME

"Her Game" is pretty much coming from the opposite extreme of "On and On." It's a reflection of my old days again, a song based on an imaginary encounter between two people who can't really connect because both are after their own self-gratification. You could call it an anthem on the endless pursuit of selfish desires.

The song gets specific, but it's not about any particular person. It's more a composite of the type of woman who likes to play games, leading a guy on just to shut him down. (It could, of course, equally apply to a man who plays games with women.) When you're young and your heart is more open, that kind of romantic cat-and-mouse can be very damaging, even though it may seem frivolous or fun to the person who is putting you through it. In my experience, when you're playing with someone's emotions, it usually means that, in some way, you're damaged goods and someone else, somewhere down the line, has treated you the same way.

Of course, if you're letting yourself be toyed with, fluttering around that dangerous person like a moth to the flame, then you're asking for whatever you get. The song tries to see it from both points of view. Yet it leaves the listener with a hopeful message: you have to learn from your mistakes. Don't give up on love just because you've been hurt. Pick yourself up, dust yourself off, and get back into the race.

> "I don't make it a policy to hide from my mistakes."

As you can probably tell from this book, I don't make it a policy to hide from my mistakes. When I mess up in a given situation, either professionally or personally, I'm sometimes reminded of the life of Christ and how He avoided mistakes by being aware of the circumstances He faced and what was in the hearts of people He encountered. It's that kind of awareness I'd like to cultivate so that if I really can't avoid making mistakes, at least I don't always have to learn the hard way.

Dragons, Wizards, and Trolls

Several songs on this album are about learning the hard way because I think that's a common experience for most people. The relationship described in a song such as "Her Game" was drawn from that lost and meandering part of my life when I was caught up in trying to find something that I couldn't even describe to myself, much less to anyone else. I was searching for my sense of identity, and I poured into those tracks the frustration I was feeling at not being able to lay hold of the truth about who I was.

Subsequent songs such as "Shaping Space," "Be," and "Existence" reflect some of the answers I have found, both in my career with dc Talk and in the growth process I have undergone in my marriage. In that way I think this album completes a full circle. It's a journey, and as the poet T. S. Eliot said, the purpose of a journey is to return to the place where you started and be able to recognize it for the first time.

As I noted earlier, one of my favorite authors is J. R. R. Tolkien, and in *The Hobbit* he writes about a small, defenseless creature heading out on an epic, heroic journey, battling dragons and wizards and trolls. In the end, when he comes through his adventure, he returns to his little house where it all began.

It's a great example of the life I'd like to live, to go out and achieve important and challenging goals, not just to be victorious, but also to be able to apply what I've learned in everyday life.

I've come a long way since I wrote "Her Game," and in some aspects I'm a completely different person from the one described in the song. I had to face my dragons and trolls, and now, looking back, I can clearly see how those battles lost and won have shaped my life today. It's a process that continues to the moment we die if we allow ourselves to stay open and teachable.

Like this chapter, the message of "Her Game" is simple and direct. We need to deal with each other the way we want to be dealt with. Nobody likes to be the pawn in somebody else's game, and although the world is ready to teach us all kinds of slick moves to get what we want, God is looking for honesty, sincerity, and transparency.

Kevin on a family trip to Israel in early 1984
(Ride 'em, London cowboy!)

Track
Thirteen

DECONSTRUCTING VENUS

You are the center of your own private little
    constellation
And you are the jury and judge of every
    little deconstructed fable
And you like the way it is
You don't want to question it
You're the wonder of God's own handiwork

Yeah, you wear Versace, but you look like a dirty bird
And yeah, even the paparazzi think you're quite absurd

Venus of your own consent, is there anything you give
    up for Lent?
Oh parasite, oh peacock of pride, will you let the little
    people see inside you?
And you don't wanna question it
And you're looking quite possessed
You're the wonder of God's own handiwork

Yeah, you wear Versace, but you look like a . . .
And yeah, even the buying public thinks
   you're quite a jerk

And you're trapped in your little castle
Like Randolph Hearst in his fringe and tassel
Yeah, you wear Versace, but you look like a . . .
And yeah, even the paparazzi think you're quite absurd

There's too much information on the television
Innocent we have been sprung and innocent we are
You don't know how to feel, you don't know
This is the eye of the storm
This is society

DECONSTRUCTING VENUS

While "Deconstructing Venus" comes from the same time and touches on some of the same themes as tracks such as "Her Game" and "Blind," it comes from a completely different point of view. The central character is a woman who finds herself in a situation most people dream about, being a successful model or film star or TV personality who's got it all—except the wisdom not to get caught up in her own hype.

I've run into a lot of hopeful young celebrity wanna-bes during my time in the music business. Many of them have ascended quickly up the ladder of success and notoriety, and from the outside they seem to have everything going for them. But on the inside it's a whole different story. They're lonely and insecure and tortured by their feelings of worthlessness. In "Deconstructing Venus" that internal contradiction has reached a level so intense that the character can no longer hide her misery; it becomes so apparent that even the outside world starts to see it.

People in positions of power who don't have a strong sense of themselves beyond the image that is created around them have nothing to hang on to when that public persona begins to lose its luster. Some of them can be very creative and intriguing, but they don't have the self-confidence to resist the role playing that others want them to assume, and they eventually become caricatures of themselves, homogenized plastic creations churned out by the dream factories of the entertainment industry.

We've become victims of our all-consuming media fascination, mesmerized by the styles and trends that pass for creative innovation. We've lost the ability to appreciate what's real, and it's a blindness that extends to the celebrities we worship. They are no longer human, but only projections of our fantasies, which, in turn, are fed by movies and music, videos and tabloids, and all the other distractions that fill our lives.

"We're surrounded by junk culture, without depth or substance, lacking in thought or spirituality."

We're surrounded by junk culture, without depth or substance, lacking in thought or spirituality. It's no wonder that when celebrities and would-be celebrities buy into that lie, they lose touch with themselves and any connection with the real world. As long as they're basking in the spotlight, they can keep away the fear and alienation, but once the public's attention fades—as it always does—they're left empty and forgotten, used up and tossed away like some disposable distraction, a bright bauble that has lost its luster. "Do not love the world nor the things in the world," the apostle wrote in 1 John 2:15–16. "If anyone loves the world, the love of the Father is not in him. For all that is in the world, the lust of the flesh and the lust of the eyes and the boastful pride of life, is not from the Father."

Marilyn Manson and Eminem

The character in the song isn't real, but one section of the chorus was inspired by an actual and very well-known event. When I sing, "You wear Versace but you look like a dirty bird," I was thinking of the awards show when Jennifer Lopez let it all hang out in that Versace dress. Such a big deal was made about her willingness to expose herself in that way that it eclipsed everything else that happened that night and for weeks to come. To me, that's a grim indication of how far we've sunk into a vicarious, voyeuristic existence in this society. It's a sign of our times, and I can't help wondering what it's saying about us.

Before I was married, I dated a model in New York City for a brief interlude. She was well on her way to the kind of success that comes with beautiful looks and naked ambition, but there was something sad and pathetic about a lifestyle that consisted solely of trying to look good with the right people in the right places. It was all about outward appearances and externals. There was nothing behind the gorgeous mask, and yet she believed she was attaining some ideal that set her apart and made her special. She was a victim of the illusions that are bought and sold on a mass scale every day by the dark forces holding the levers of power in this world.

> *"The battle for truth is being fought on many fronts."*

Of course, acknowledging that this world is in the grip of evil doesn't mean that God isn't ultimately in control. Even in the realm of entertainment He uses all kinds of people to get His work done. I think He even uses Marilyn Manson to prod people to think about Him and the choices they have to make in this life to follow Him or turn away.

As controversial artists, Eminem and others like him are serving their purpose by asking questions as opposed to providing answers. Trying to censor them for the questions they're posing is setting up society for trouble. The minute that happens, the minute society tries to stop people from saying what they want to say, they just go underground and start their own subculture. Hard-core rap may be a perversion of our right to free expression, and maybe those artists are pushing their freedoms in our faces, but there are always going to be people who buy their message, no matter how irresponsible it may be. It's just a matter of time before someone even more outrageous than Eminem gets out there, but that's part of the function of real art in any culture.

Artists are supposed to push the envelope, as much as to depict beauty or inspire and challenge us. They reflect what's happening around them, even if all they're doing is giving people who don't have a lot of security in themselves something to grab on to. I can't say if that's a good thing or a bad thing, but I do know that even artists like Eminem are part of God's big picture—if it's only to bring us to the point where we realize we've had enough of violence and self-hatred. God uses all of us, and to think that He can't is to take away from the power of who He is.

The battle for truth is being fought on many fronts, not the least of which is the music business itself. Too many artists are afraid to be different, and too many executives are afraid to take risks. Music, the art form I love and have dedicated my life to, is in danger of becoming irrelevant as a cultural force. If I can accomplish anything in my career, I hope that I can make music interesting again. I hope that, when people buy my record, they'll take it home, close the doors to their rooms, slip on their headphones, and really let it take them away. That's how music used to affect me, and I want to have that same effect on my audience. A supernova burns brightly in the night, and then it's gone, never to return. I'm interested in sticking around for the long haul because I truly believe, for me and for all of us, that the best is yet to come.

If you believe that, too, you're a long way down the road we all have to travel to come to the place God has set aside for us. He wants to bless us, and if we can hang on to that fact and let it sink deep into our hearts, our lives will be enriched, no matter how many years have been allotted to us.

Halloween party at the Max residence
Yeah, baby, Yeah!

Track
Fourteen

I WENT OVER THE EDGE OF THE WORLD

Oh the hymns of angels
Suffer over the stench of the twenty-first century
Nothing is black or white
Or devoid of industry
The face of monotony
The litany of popular culture
I face the microphone and fumble in my pockets
       for a change
A break from the deranged world of
Plotting out the death of art

And I went over the edge of the world
And felt the sting of all its words
I sang the song of elves and birds
I saw you in my rearview shades
And drank from pools of nighttime cafés
I stopped over just to finish up
I turned the knobs and called your bluff
I went over the edge of the world
I face the microphone and fumble in my pockets
    for change
A break from the deranged world of
Plotting out the death of art

I WENT OVER THE EDGE OF THE WORLD

I've said before that my album is supposed to take the listener on a journey and that the journey eventually comes full circle, back to the place it started. The same is true of this book.

These pages began with my comments about how most artists are reluctant to describe the intent and content of their music. "The song says it all," they'll tell you if you try to push them too hard. I can relate to that, but I also wanted to give my audience and now my readers some insight into what my songs mean to me and how they express the issues that I think are critical, not just to our society, but to our souls.

But now that we've come to the last track, a poem set to a melody called "I Went Over the Edge of the World," I've got the feeling that maybe I should just let this one speak for itself. Any song is only as good as the impact it makes on the listener.

The Best That You Can Be

I could tell you that "I Went Over the Edge of the World" describes my feelings as I step out on my own as a solo artist for the first time. I could tell you it's about leaving behind the security I've known to take a risk with no guarantee of success. I could tell you it's about moving out from the shadow of dc Talk or reaching for something more real in my marriage to Alayna.

But I'm not going to tell you any of that. I'm interested in what *you* think this last track is about. Because maybe it could be more meaningful to you than it is to me. Maybe you know the free-falling sensation that comes when you dare to believe you are meant for something special. Maybe God wants you to hear a unique message in this song.

> "Maybe you know the *free-falling* sensation that comes when you dare to believe you are meant for something special."

I sure wouldn't want to spoil that. Part of my being who I am, and your being who you are, comes from the way we see the world around us. Our individual points of view are completely unique, never before experienced and never to be duplicated. I guess leaving this last song dangling is my way of encouraging you to take a step off the edge, to believe that you are meant to discover the truth and pass it along. What's waiting over there on the other side? That's a mystery.

God's mystery.

A mystery called *you*.

Check out These Other Groovy Products from Extreme for Jesus

Bibles

The Extreme Teen Bible [NKJV]

Hardcover	$24.99	0-7852-0081-9
Paperback	$19.99	0-7852-0082-7
Black Bonded Leather	$39.99	0-7852-5555-9
Deep Purple Bonded Leather	$39.99	0-7852-5525-7
Slimey Limey Green Bonded Leather	$39.99	0-7852-5646-6
Lava Orange Bonded Leather	$39.99	0-7852-5678-4

The Gospel of John

The Gospel of John	$1.50	0-7852-5537-0

Extreme Word Bible [NKJV]

Paperback	$19.99	0-7852-5732-2
Pitch-Black Bonded Leather	$39.99	0-7852-5735-7
Chromium Hardcover	$29.99	0-7852-5733-0
Blue Snake Hardcover	$29.99	0-7852-5796-9

The Extreme Teen Bible [NCV]

Paperback	$19.99	0-7852-5834-5
Hardcover	$24.99	0-7852-5835-3
Retread Grey	$39.99	0-7180-0063-3
Reigncoat Vinyl	$39.99	0-7180-0062-5

Books

Extreme A-Z: Find it in the Bible	$19.99	0-7852-4580-4
Extreme Answers to Extreme Questions	$12.99	0-7852-4594-4
Extreme Journey: Get More Out of It	$14.99	0-7852-4595-2
The Dictionary: Meaning in God's Words	$19.99	0-7852-4611-8
Burn—Live the Compassion of Jesus	$9.99	0-7852-6746-8
Genuine, by Stacie Orrico (with CD)	$13.99	0-8499-9545-0
Extreme Faith	$10.99	0-7852-6757-3
God's Promises Rock (Your World)	$3.99	0-8499-9507-8
Extreme for Jesus Promise Book	$13.99	0-8499-5606-4
Fuel—Igniting Your Life with Passionate Prayer	$12.99	0-7852-6748-4

Devotionals

30 Days With Jesus	$7.99	0-7852-6626-5
Extreme Encounters	$9.99	0-7852-5657-1

Workbook

Step Off: Hardest 30 Days	$19.99	0-7852-4604-5

Journals

Xt4J Journal, Plastic Cover	$9.99	0-8499-5710-9
Xt4J Journal, Spiral bound hardcover	$9.99	0-8499-9508-6

Calendar

No Repeat Days	$9.99	0-8499-9510-8